D1728145

OTHER BOOKS BY
CARRIE JANE KNOWLES

The Last Childhood:
A Family Story of Alzheimer's
Lillian's Garden
Ashoan's Rug
A Garden Wall in Provence
Black Tie Optional: 17 Stories
A Self-guided Workbook
and Gentle Tour on How to Write
Stories From Start to Finish
The Inevitable Past
A Musical Affair

COLUMNIST
Psychology Today: Shifting Forward
psychologytoday.com/shifting-forward

SHIFTING
FORWARD
Fifty Reflections on Everyday Life

SHIFTING
FORWARD

Fifty Reflections on Everyday Life

Carrie Jane Knowles

OWL CANYON
PRESS

BOULDER, COLORADO

First Edition, 2022
All Rights Reserved
Library of Congress Cataloging-in-Publication Data

Knowles, Carrie Jane
Shifting Forward: Fifty Reflections on Everyday Life —1st ed.
p. cm.

ISBN: 978-1-952085-15-4
Library of Congress Control Number: 2021950474

Owl Canyon Press
Boulder, Colorado

Disclaimer

DEDICATION

To our grandchildren:
Aiden, Jack, Lily, Rex and Esme.

ACKNOWLEDGEMENTS

The essays in this collection were first published online in *Psychology Today*'s Personal Perspectives section.

I would like to thank my editor at *Psychology Today*, Lybi Ma, for asking me to write *Shifting Forward* and believing good things would come from it.

CONTENTS

INTRODUCTION

When I started writing for *Psychology Today*, my editor, Lybi Ma, asked what I wanted to call my column. My directive from her was to write a personal perspectives column not as a psychologist (which I'm not) but as a life observer and writer.

Given free rein to explore a wide range of topics, I liked the idea of writing about moving in a positive direction to something more purposeful in our lives. I decided to call the column: *Shifting Forward*.

Both Lybi and I agreed this title set a tone for the column and provided a framework for exploring numerous themes related to moving forward in our lives.

Neither of us had any inkling, when the first column was published in August of 2018, that in just a few short months, we would all be caught in the collective experience of COVID 19: wearing masks, working virtually from home, home schooling, ordering groceries online, and attending Zoom meetings half dressed in our pajamas.

My first column, "On Purpose," told the story of our then two-year-old granddaughter, Lily, learning the difference between accidentally doing something and doing it on purpose. But you know how columns go: they start one place and take you to quite another by the end. In this case, the article took a sweet left turn into making life decisions regarding what you want to do with your life as you age, rather than just letting things happen.

Things happen when you least expect it. And, when you shift forward, you need to know where you're going. It's also good to know why you're going there.

Over the last three years, I have written more than fifty columns about a wide range of subjects: Alzheimer's, downsizing, grey hair, fashion rules and why we shouldn't care, summer tomatoes, holidays, winter gardens, wildfires, traveling, learning to sit still, the whiplash of politics in our divided country, and dozens of other odd, soul-searching, everyday ideas. Oh yeah, and COVID.

I have written a lot about our lives in COVID. Not only what we were dealing with while being quarantined, but what things we might want to change once we begin to rebuild our work and home lives in a less confined way.

Several years before COVID, a tornado blew through an historic cemetery that had been established in 1795 at the then edge of downtown Raleigh and managed to lay waste to a great number of trees and ancient tombstones. Just months before the storm, the cemetery, which happens to be near my office, was declared a National Historic Site. During the application process, trees were trimmed, tombstones restored, grounds spruced-up and the original iron fence surrounding the four-acre cemetery mended.

In a few short minutes, the tornado that touched down in the cemetery uprooted trees, tore down the beautifully restored fence, and damaged the newly cleaned and restored headstones.

After the fallen trees were removed and debris cleared, a professional crew, trained in the restoration of historic sites, came to repair the damage caused by the storm. However, given the National Historic Registry designation of the property, they could only repair and restore the mausoleums and grave markers that had been documented as whole before the tornado had hit.

Markers that had been whole before the tornado but were now chipped or broken by the storm could be repaired, but those that had been broken before, and were documented as such, were to be cleaned, put back in place, but not repaired.

The workers used photographs and diagrams that had been made during the application for the National Historic Registry to guide their repairs. The work was slow and tedious, but no one seemed in a hurry. They had a job to do, and it was clear they believed it needed to be done right.

I was fascinated by their careful repairs and the reverence they showed for the job they were performing.

While the restoration work went on, I walked through the cemetery every afternoon to see the progress they were making. There was something very fascinating about the skill and respect they showed for the task at hand, and the lives that had been lost and some forgotten.

One afternoon, toward the end of the repairs, I found two of the cleanup crew sitting on upturned five-gallon plastic buckets, gently scrubbing away storm dirt from the last few, fragile tombstones. These markers were in a far southeast section of the cemetery noted in the plot map of the grounds as being reserved for "Negroes and persons of color", i.e., slaves and servants of the wealthy individuals buried in the more prominent north section of the graveyard.

The workers were used to my afternoon wanderings and looked up to acknowledge my presence as I approached but didn't stop what they were doing.

I knew that cleaning up this last bit of the cemetery meant that they would soon be done and on their way to another job. As one of the men dipped his scrub brush into a bucket of water and gently worked through the soft grooves of the inscription on the tombstone he was cleaning, I asked him if he had enjoyed making the repairs and restoring the cemetery.

"It's good work to do," he said. Then he went back to his task at hand.

I was struck by his earnest reply and his statement that it was good work. That what he was doing mattered. That it made a difference.

Here's what I've learned while both living through COVID and writing these columns: making changes in our lives and deciding to shift forward in a positive way is challenging...but it is good work to do.

Our lives matter. What we do makes a difference.

PART ONE

IT'S ALL
ABOUT LIVING
WITH PURPOSE

It's Time to Decide to Live with Purpose Rather Than Letting Things Happen.

When our granddaughter Lily was two years old, she carefully considered her options regarding toilet training: Should she embrace the discipline of big girl panties, or should she continue with the easy convenience of diapers? There were pros and cons with either option. It was a tough decision.

Lily is an enthusiastic lover of books, so our daughter bought her a Sesame Street book about toilet training in hopes of urging her along the journey of becoming a Big Girl.

In the Sesame Street book, the young Albie is just beginning the toilet training process and is quite proud to be wearing big boy pants. All is well until Elmo comes over and Albie gets so caught up playing with his friend that he has an accident.

Albie's mother wisely tells him not to worry about having an accident, that sometimes things just happen.

Lily immediately grabbed the concept that things happen and ran with it.

That night at dinner, when Lily spilled her milk because she forgot to hold onto her cup with two hands, she turned to her mother and said: "Happens!"

When she didn't want to eat her sandwich and dropped it instead on the floor so the dog could eat it, she looked at her mother, smiled and said: "Happens!"

Numerous things began to "happen" in their home, so a few days later, her father sat Lily down on the couch next to him and had a long talk with her regarding the difference between those things that are accidents, and just "happen" and those things we choose to do on purpose.

Lily listened carefully.

When her father finished, she slid off the couch, picked up a toy and threw it as hard as she could across the room. Then she turned to her father and boldly announced, "On purpose!"

No apologies. Just a matter of fact. She was fully conscious of what she had done. She threw the toy on purpose. She knew what she was doing. There was no accident in it.

She got it.

Wow.

When accidents happen in Lily's world, she is quick to get over them and move on.

As for those things she chooses to do on purpose—well, she thinks about them, makes up her mind to do them, does them, and does not stop to apologize for any of it.

Lily's father told me it was all he could do to keep from laughing when she picked up the toy and threw it across the room, "On purpose!"

I must confess I would have laughed, and probably would have applauded as well. I loved that she did not feel a need to apologize for her actions.

It is easy to live a life where things just happen because, like Albie, we are not paying attention to what we should be doing. Believing we don't have the time to pay attention to every little detail swirling around us gives us an excuse to lead a less than purposeful life.

I watched my mother and her friends let life happen and carry them along, way past the time when they could safely care for themselves. Their children then had to step in and take on the role of caretaker as well as sort through a lifetime of belongings in the home, throwing things away, packing up mementos for family members, carrying stuff to the Goodwill, and deciding what should move on to an independent living unit, assisted living or nursing home.

I wanted to make my own decisions about how my life would spin out. That's why I pushed for us to downsize. Some of our friends thought it was too early to make such a move, but I didn't care. Our decision to downsize had nothing to do with them.

When we moved, we freed ourselves of stuff, gave things to our children that they wanted, and now have the pleasure of seeing how they have incorporated our things and memories into their own lives.

There is beauty in living with purpose.

No apologies need apply.

Could You Travel With Less and Enjoy the Journey More?

We once took an extended, three-week vacation in Greece. Neither one of us spoke a word of Greek, so we booked a ten-day archeological tour, in English, of the Peloponnese in order to get familiar with the country and its history before venturing out on our own.

As we assembled on the first morning to board the bus, I noticed one stately older woman standing alone without luggage. I asked if we could help her get her bags from the hotel.

She smiled, lifted her purse, and told us that her purse was all she was carrying. She said she never burdened her travels with luggage. Instead, she went to the markets on the first stop on any tour and bought several outfits from local vendors. When she is ready to return home, she has the clothes she bought laundered and ironed and leaves them for the hotel housekeepers.

"I have fun buying local clothing and blending in," she explained. "I carry my underwear, personal items and a little nylon tote for my purchases in my purse. It's the best way to travel."

She never burdened her travels with luggage. I think she was on to something.

At the end of our trip that summer, we stayed at a very small hotel in Crete. Our room was on the third floor. There was no elevator. To get to our room, we had to walk up an extremely narrow spiral staircase balancing our heavy luggage on our heads!

Traveling unburdened, or at least lighter, was gaining traction with me. Once home, I bought a smaller piece of luggage and afterward, tried my best to take only one checked bag and one carry-on when we went on vacation.

If I couldn't carry my luggage myself, or balance it on my head, I needed to lighten my load.

Slide forward a couple of dozen years.

For many years, the weight limit on checked luggage for overseas travel was 70 pounds with a two-bag allowance. Then it dropped to 50 pounds for both domestic and international flights. Shortly after that, many airlines started charging for the second checked bag. Then, several airlines began charging for all checked luggage, and now many of the discount airlines charge for carry-on as well as checked bags.

I'm not so sure that it's a bad thing.

Could you travel for a week with only a carry-on? How about with just a personal item like a large purse or a briefcase? FYI, a personal item must not be bigger than 18" x 16" x 8", (8" being the maximum thickness that can easily slide under the seat in front of you): plenty of room for underwear and a couple of changes of clothing. It can work if you wear your raincoat and sweater and comfortable shoes on the plane and pack only a few clothes that can be hand washed and hung up to dry in your hotel room, preferably clothing that can take you from a walking tour to dinner.

As for that issue with the TSA and toiletries, short of medications and a favorite toothbrush, you can buy shampoo, lotion and soap in even the most remote of countries. What you don't use while you're traveling, you can leave behind in the hotel for someone else.

I've forgotten many details about our trip through the Peloponnese but have never forgotten that extraordinary woman who went boldly into the world alone with little in tow.

Could you unburden your travels of excess luggage? It's a challenge, but one that comes with certain perks. You'll be traveling with less to take care of, keep track of, lug up and down stairs, stuff into the trunk of a taxi, or drag onto a train.

Plus, there's the added benefit of a cheaper ticket, no standing in line to check bags, and no more lost luggage.

How Cats Have Helped Me Understand the Truth about Long-Term Commitments.

I have had two cats in my adult life. The first was Cleo; the second was Eleanor. Both were named after strong women: Cleopatra and Eleanor of Aquitaine, with a nod to Eleanor Roosevelt, another strong woman.

I suppose, if I ever decided to adopt a third cat, I would name her RBG or perhaps just Ginsberg for short.

But I don't think I'm going to get a third cat. It's not that I don't like or don't want another cat. It's just that the two cats I have had were long-lived. Cleo lived to be 19 years old. Eleanor lived to be 23. That's human years, not cat years. I'm not up to making that level of commitment again.

To give you some perspective on cat years versus human years: according to Catstir.com, a cat matures in the first 12 months of life, the equal of 15 human years. By the end of their second year, cats have reached the human equivalent of 24 years. Thereafter, every human year equates to four cat years. In short, Cleo lived to be 92, and Eleanor lived to be 108.

Dog years can be calculated in the same way. Our dog, Phoebe, lived to be 13 years old, or 74 in dog years. Not a bad run for a slightly overweight Basset Hound with bad knees.

Cats, unlike dogs, do not need, nor do they ever desire, to be walked. Or, for that matter, to exercise at all, which makes them slightly more low maintenance than dogs. However, cats are lawless.

You can't tell them anything. They don't do tricks. Still, they can be housebroken, even though they cannot be trained.

While vacationing in Cassis, a Mediterranean fishing port in southern France, we watched a street busker break a sweat trying to get his "World Famous Cat Circus" to perform. All he wanted his three cats to do was walk up a short wooden ladder, cross a small wooden bridge (we are talking 12-15 inches here) then jump down onto the platform/stage he had created for them to perform upon. When that trick failed, he spent another ten minutes or so trying to tempt them with bits of fish to jump through a hoop.

Despite all he offered for them to perform, the circus cats ignored him and relaxed in the warmth of the Mediterranean sunshine.

I like cats. I find their independence refreshing, their unnerving need not to please anyone admirable. Plus, they have a dedication to naps that is epic and worth emulating. Caring for a cat, however, has its challenges. Feeding a cat anything short of a freshly killed mouse is akin to trying to get a toddler to eat broccoli when he or she has a cookie in hand. But, their love of the hunt, even if it's just stalking a shadow dancing across a wall, or a buzzing fly, can be charming, as long as it doesn't involve their catching a claw in your draperies and bringing the whole mess crashing down.

So, here's what I want to say about inviting cats into your home to share your life. It's a commitment.

I'm all about commitment, but I find myself unwilling to commit to having another cat in my life/my home, kind of in the same way I'm not willing to commit to doing any number of things I don't want to do anymore.

For instance, I'm not willing to commit to ironing shirts anymore. Wrinkled is fine. I'm also not willing to commit to reading any book beyond the first fifteen pages. If it doesn't grab me by then, I move on to the next book on my nightstand. No guilt involved. Ditto with movies on Netflix. Movies get fifteen minutes of my attention before I either commit or click on down the road to something else.

As for people, I'm no longer willing to abide by narrow-minded thinking, by prejudice, by a sense of entitlement, or just plain self-centered boorishness. I'm also not willing to commit to being with people who don't accept me for who I am or who expect me to jump through hoops in order to be friends with them.

Cats have taught me a lot.

Lessons learned.

If You're Lucky, First Loves Become Best Friends Forever.

Our older son, Neil, was Anna's first love. He was thirteen and Anna was four when they met. Neil was a counselor in our neighborhood summer camp and Anna was a camper. She followed him everywhere. Anna had Down syndrome and tired easily and when she did, Neil picked her up and carried her so she could participate in everything the other campers were doing. Anna called him Big Neil.

By the time camp was over, Anna was part of our family, and we were part of hers. Neil never passed up a chance to include Anna in his life. He went out of his way to introduce her to his friends, including his girlfriends. He was proud of his friendship with her, and she of him.

When Neil went away to college, he kept in touch with Anna. When Neil brought his fiancée, Sophie, home to meet our family he wanted to introduce Sophie to Anna.

During dinner that night, Anna turned to Neil and asked: "Do you love her?"

"Yes, I do," Neil replied.

"Then I'll love her too," Anna reassured him.

Anna gave a speech at Neil's wedding and made a toast. She also claimed a dance with him.

Cole, our younger son, eventually became her second big love. Anna loved baseball. So did Cole.

After Cole started playing little league, Anna decided he should have a good baseball-player name and crowned him Chigger Bo-Bo.

When she joined the Braves team in the Miracle League, an adaptive baseball league, she claimed her own nickname: Anna Bonanza. She rarely hit a ball beyond second base but that didn't stop her from loving the game. In Miracle League, no matter how many swings it takes to hit the ball or where it falls, players always run the bases and score a homerun.

Her walk-on song was the theme from "Bonanza."

Cole and Anna were the same age, and as the birthdays ticked by, the developmental differences between Anna and Cole became more apparent, but their friendship never wavered. Just as Neil and our daughter Hedy had done, when Cole moved forward with his life, he never left Anna behind. That's not what good friends do. Not much stopped Anna from enjoying life. I can only remember one instance when she was nearly defeated by whatever limitations Down syndrome had handed her. Cole was home from college, and we were out to dinner with Anna and her family. Rather than bubbling with conversation as usual, she was withdrawn.

"What's wrong?" Cole asked.

"I'm going to fail my final exam tomorrow," she said.

Anna was in high school at the time.

"What's the class?" Cole asked.

"Gym," Anna said.

"I was good in gym," Cole said. "I bet I can help you."

"It's on the rules of badminton."

"Do you even like badminton?" Cole asked.

"No," she said emphatically.

"I don't either. No one really needs to know the rules of badminton. It's a stupid test. Let's have another garlic knot."

Anna danced at Cole's wedding and gave a toast. She spoke about how much she loved our family. She went on to say she not only had us to love she had Neil's wife Sophie and their son, Aiden. She had Hedy as well as Bill and their daughter, Lily. And now she had Cole's wife, Lital.

Friends for life no matter what.

Cole gave one of the eulogies at Anna's funeral.

Anna's sister, Caitlin was the one who called to let us know Anna had died, and I, in turn had to call our three children.

It was the hardest thing I have ever done.

Anna, like so many other individuals with Down syndrome, had congenital heart issues. Her death was unexpected and left all of us shattered and standing on broken ice in a once safe pond.

In a true friendship, each of us gives the other great gifts. Being friends and extended family with Anna taught us that we should quit worrying about the stupid things like final exams. We should eat the basket of garlic knots and sometimes ask for more. And, that we should always embrace the idea that the baseball we barely hit into the infield is, in fact, yet another home run for our lives.

Most importantly, that knowing the rules of badminton has little or nothing to do with love or living a rich life.

Have You Ever Scurryfunged? What's Hiding in Your Closet?

Is that the sports jacket you wore to your cousin's Bar Mitzvah in 1962 stuffed into the back of your closet?

Are those the red four-inch heels you bought to wear for your best friend's wedding… in 2000? They hurt your feet then. Have you worn them since?

How about your once favorite brown sweater? The one you wore almost every day when you were a freshman in college. The very same one the moths have munched on for the last 10 years. Do you still wear that? Any chance you're saving it for your next camping trip? Do you still camp?

Like everyone else you know, your closet is jam-packed with your past: the fun you had, the mistakes you made. The good, the bad, and the ugly moth-eaten sweater.

Let's face it: Closets are dangerous. They have doors. Things can get lost in your closet. No matter how good your intentions of one day dressing up again as your old self, your bell-bottomed, gypsy-skirted, and platform-shoed-lives stubbornly cling to those closets as reminders of glory days past.

Past. Not present.

Remember the time when you rushed home from work to make dinner because your in-laws were coming? That afternoon when you didn't have time to clean, so you did a quick pick-up and tossed magazines, shoes, hats, scarves, and dirty gym clothes into the closet and closed the door? Are those things still in there? Maybe.

By the way, in the 19th century, the common word for that kind of hurry-up-and-hide cleaning process was called scurryfunge. It was used to describe a hasty tidying when a guest was coming, as in, I scurryfunge every time my mother-in-law comes for dinner.

It seems that the impulse to throw things in the closet to get them out of sight has been around for a long time.

All closets harbor secrets, but by far, the most frightening closets in any house are the ones that don't have lights in them. Dark closets are the places where mittens get lost, unloved books get tossed, and broken luggage gets stored. The smaller the closet, the bigger the problem. No one, not even the dog, wants to rummage around in the dust-encrusted bottom of a small dark closet looking for a smelly lost sneaker.

As we all know, if we are being honest with ourselves, big closets, even well-lit ones, are an open invitation to keep things that are WAY past their use-by date.

We have owned two turn-of-the-century homes. Both came sans closets. So, we built closets. Decent sized ones. Not our wisest decision.

What would our lives be like today if we had never built those closets? Perhaps we would have been forced to hang all our clothing inside small wooden wardrobes, with our shoes paired neatly on the floor beside the bed. If we had been forced, by not having any closets, to only own/wear/ keep what would fit into that tidy bit of bedroom furniture, I'm willing to bet our lives would be tidier.

Closets, however, are often not the worst offenders in the world of scurryfunging.

If you own an attic or a basement or even a storage unit, your life of gathering and keeping stuff will be forever doomed. How can you get rid of something if you have a place to store it?

I'm ready to clean out the past and shut the door on closets. How about you?

Enough keeping.

It's time to let go.

Time to stop saving those things that are too tight or just plain too useless or ugly to keep.

It's time to make some breathing room in your closets, your home, and your life.

Tired of Multi-Tasking? Why Not Give Life-Guarding a Try?

I get up three times a week and push myself to do an hour workout at the local pool. It's a deep-water aerobics class. My theory, and it's a good one, is that you can't really hurt yourself in the water: i.e., you can't sprain an ankle or a knee, chip a tooth, or skin an elbow while "running" around in the deep water.

This morning, in the middle of the class, I happened to look up and notice the lifeguard. He was just sitting there, elbows on his knees, intently watching as we stretched, kicked, and paddled our way from one side of the pool to the other.

This is what he always does, but what struck me this morning was that he wasn't doing anything else. He wasn't multi-tasking. He wasn't reading a book, talking on the phone, checking his text messages, looking at his calendar to see if he could meet with someone in the afternoon, paying a bill or answering a question. He wasn't doing anything but his job: watching us, making sure we were safe.

He was, in the truest sense of the word, life-guarding, i.e., taking care to live in the moment and be fully engaged with the task at hand.

Funny what you can miss when you are constantly working in overdrive mode, doing what you always do, not stopping to think about what is going on right in front of you.

Although in the five years I have been doing water aerobics, there has never been a situation where the lifeguard needed to jump from his or her tower to rescue one of us, I was grateful he was there this morning. Instead of rescuing me from drowning, he saved me, for that moment, from thinking about anything but exercising and getting stronger.

Imagine how different we would feel if we spent the day life-guarding rather than multi-tasking.

Not so quick…and not so easy, you say. Multi-tasking seems to be what's expected of us as employees, parents, or just modern-day people. It is not enough anymore to do one thing at a time and do it well.

In the demanding get-it-all-done-and-dinner-on-the-table world we live in, our attention is rarely focused. It is always being stretched and tugged upon.

Does it have to be?

What if we resisted the temptation to do it all and just stopped multi-tasking? Cold turkey. No excuses.

What if we turned off our cell phones, pushed away from our computers, and quelled those screeching voices in our heads that are always shouting shoulds and coulds every minute we attempt to slow down? What if we pretended that the most important thing for us to be doing at any given moment is just *one* thing? It wouldn't matter if the thing we were concentrating on was swimming laps, meeting a deadline at work, trying to explain fractions to one of our children, fixing dinner, or having a cup of coffee with a friend.

It wouldn't matter what task was at hand. What would matter would be that all, yes, *all* of our attention would be on that one thing and nothing else.

When our children were still at home and I was juggling being a writer/wife/mother while at the same time trying to get dinner on the table, I got caught and called out by our three children for not being truly present. They were right. While I was stirring the soup and answering homework questions, I was thinking about a paragraph that needed to be rewritten or my next assignment.

I was not present.

I was physically there but thinking about something other than the task at hand.

In a nutshell, that's what multi-tasking does: it takes us off the very task that is in front of us. The task I was escaping from by thinking about what I thought I needed to do for that article was the task of being with my children.

Truth is, I should not have even been stirring the soup or wondering if I needed to add a pinch more salt to the broth. I should have pushed aside the assignment I was working on, put the spoon down and paid attention to them. I should have been connected to the moment.

I should have been life-guarding.

If Disaster Struck, Could You Start Over?

Wildfires. The loss of your home to a natural disaster: a hurricane, tsunami, flood, volcanic eruption, or an earthquake. War. Famine. Fear for the safety of your children. Drought. Ethnic cleansing. Mass genocide.

There are many reasons to pack your things and leave in the middle of the night. You don't have to be poor to seek asylum. You just have to be in a bad place.

Wealthy homeowners from Los Angeles to Sonoma County were recently told to be packed and ready to abandon their homes and go on a moment's notice as the latest California fires burned their way through gardens and golf courses, vineyards, shopping centers and cul-de-sacs, highways and hillsides.

Packed and ready to go. But what do you take? What would you save from the fire?

My husband's parents left Germany just before WWII. They not only had to leave their homes and possessions, but their country as well. At that time, it was illegal for German Jews to take any money out of the country. They could, however, take household goods and clothing. Consequently, we inherited thirty monogrammed damask linen tablecloths: some used, some brand new.

What, beyond lending the tablecloths to friends and fundraising events, were we going to do with thirty damask linen tablecloths? We eventually distributed them amongst our children and my husband's cousins and their children.

We also inherited a set of gold rimmed Hutschenreuther bone china, service for twelve, and a set of German silverware.

If the wildfires were burning through our backyard, if we were facing famine, flooding, or fearing for our lives and the lives of our children, would I pack those dishes and the silverware into our car?

I don't think so.

What would I take? What do we own that would provide a sense of identity, or of comfort? What do we own that would help us make a new life somewhere else?

For sure, I would pack passports and other forms of identification. I'd grab those important documents that prove we have money in bank accounts and investments. Money is always a good thing to bring along when you are faced with starting over.

There are stories of refugees carrying seeds to plant so they will have food to eat when they settle into their new homes. I don't have seeds. Most urban dwellers don't have gardens large enough or abundant enough to provide seeds for a new beginning. Instead, we carry plastic credit cards.

But here's the question: Will our credit cards still work? Will we have enough money in our accounts to be able to make a fresh start in a new world? Would we be better off carrying seeds?

I'd grab comfortable clothes and sensible walking shoes. We would have to leave anything fancy or fanciful behind. I'd also grab a blanket or two and some pillows. Is our car big enough? How much can it carry?

We would also need food that doesn't need to be refrigerated or cooked, and lots and lots of water. We won't get very far or go very long without drinking water.

Our children and grandchildren would need those things that bring them comfort: a favorite toy, a collection of baseball cards, colored pencils, and books to read. Anything requiring batteries or electricity would have to be left behind, that is, except for cell phones. We'd need cell phones as well as phone chargers so they could be juiced up. Might be wise to have a solar powered battery pack.

As the natural disasters get bigger and more frequent, not to mention the political unrest that is rocking the world around us, the prospect of being faced with having to evacuate, to pack our cars and leave is getting all too real.

It is hard to imagine being refugees. Having to flee our home, our livelihood, our earthly possessions, and walk away with nothing but what we can carry because our lives are no longer safe. That scenario seems farfetched and unimaginable for most of us living in the United States.

But, what about fire? An earthquake? Hurricane? Tornado? Flooding?

What do we own that is essential? What identifies and defines our lives? What can we live without? What would we pack? What would we leave behind?

It's worth thinking about. The world is rapidly changing.

How Helping Someone Can Change Your Life.

It is well established that reaching out to help someone also helps the helper.

Peggy Payne, co-author with Allan Luks of *The Healing Power of Doing Good: The Health and Spiritual Benefits of Helping Others*, has this to say about helping:

"First it creates a 'helper's high,' a rush of good feeling that sets off a sharp reduction in stress and releases the body's natural painkillers, the endorphins, which is then followed by a longer period of improved emotional well-being."

The kind of help author Peggy Payne is talking about, however, requires more than baking a casserole.

I was once the sort of person who thought baking a casserole was the best way to help, until I saw a neighbor getting off a bus near her home with her groceries in tow.

The neighbor was a good friend. Let's call her Ingrid, because that was her name. Her family did not own a car. It was not a matter of money, but rather a philosophical stance that using public transportation was better than having thousands of cars crowding the roads and fouling the air.

A couple of days before, I had taken Ingrid for her initial visit with an oncologist. She had been diagnosed with breast cancer and needed someone to drive her to the appointment and take notes while the doctor explained the results of her tests, outlined her treatment options, and talked seriously about her prognosis.

The initial prognosis was grim.

I knew what Ingrid was facing and realized she shouldn't be going to the grocery store on the bus.

When I got home, I called her and offered to take her shopping on Saturday mornings, when I ran my own errands. It was an easy offer to make and, frankly, no big deal.

It did, however, change my life.

That was 32 years ago: too many rounds of chemotherapy, one pregnancy (mine, our third child), a divorce (hers), along with five high school and college graduations, five marriages/weddings, and the births of seven grandchildren among the two of us, a couple of downsizing moves, and count-less birthdays and other celebrations. Not to mention about 1,400 Saturday shopping trips and breakfasts together when we were both in town.

I wish I could tell you exactly the moment when our shopping trips seg-ued into breakfast and wandering, but I'm pretty sure it didn't take us long. Every Saturday was another gift, and it just made sense to treat it as such.

One Saturday before Ingrid died, she said: "You know, we never once asked anyone permission for our Saturdays. What in the world made us think we deserved them?"

Her remark startled me. As women/wives/mothers, we have a tendency to apologize way too quickly and just as quickly think we need to ask permis-sion to do something that does not involve our families.

Our Saturdays together had no preconceived plans or particular time schedules. We had things to do, like buying groceries and running errands that gave our wanderings some air of legitimacy, but other than that, we con-sidered ourselves, without question, free to do whatever we pleased.

I might have thought, when I made that first phone call, that I was do-ing something to help Ingrid, but I quickly understood that whatever help I thought I was offering her was bigger than a casserole. Much bigger. It changed my life.

I woke up the day she died overwhelmed with gratitude for those 1,400-plus Saturdays. I was sad, but I couldn't help but marvel at what a richness of memories and the magical power of wandering that was mine because of her.

After I helped her sons write her obituary, I got out all the bits and scraps of fabric I had from baby quilts we had made together—remnants we bought on our Saturdays for no other reason than we liked the color or the pattern of the fabric—and the odd quilt blocks we'd picked up at yard sales, unfinished work another woman had left behind.

While condolences poured in, I sewed the bits and pieces of fabric to-gether into a wild assortment of unmatched placemats.

I didn't quite know what I was going to do come the next Saturday morn-ing, but I knew for sure I wanted to have Ingrid at our table for as long as I possibly could.

Can Someone Steal Your Joy?

When you least expect it, something or someone comes along to knock you off your game and challenge you. If you take a step back to think about how you feel rather than a step forward to confront the situation, your reaction and subsequent response can not only change the course of what you're doing but also make you more aware, more grounded in your life.

We live in a condominium complex with a shared community garden. For the last nine years, my husband and I have been informally in charge of the garden. Several years ago, after many failed attempts to grow a decent tomato, the group of community gardeners met and decided to change the purpose of the garden from growing a few vegetables, all readily available in the supermarkets and at the nearby farmers' market, to growing herbs and flowers, for the whole community whether they work in the garden or not.

It was a good decision. By making this change, everyone in the community had fresh, organically grown herbs for cooking and flowers to cut. We grew rosemary, thyme, oregano, three kinds of mint, two kinds of sage, tarragon, lemon balm, lemongrass, chives, sweet and hot peppers, basil, dill, and fennel. In the cutting garden, we had a beautiful stand of Shasta daisies, Russian sage, coreopsis, coneflowers, a stunning butterfly bush to encourage pollination, ageratum, marigolds, three colors of yarrow, a dozen different colors of coleus, cockscomb, daffodils, and a couple of dozen other flowering plants. There was always something ready and available to fill a vase.

Then, one weekend while we were out of town, someone in the community came along, without asking permission, and dug up the herbs and most of the flowers so they could plant tomatoes.

Nine years of careful work was destroyed. The herb garden was gone.

What this person had so carelessly done hurt anyone who had ever worked in the garden, along with everyone who had ever cooked a meal using the herbs we grew or had cut a few flowers for their table.

We left the next weekend, both because we had planned to be away, and also because I couldn't stay home. I needed time to think about what the garden had meant to me.

Joni Mitchell's 1970s hit song, "Big Yellow Taxi" kept playing in my head, especially the one line: "You don't know what you've got 'til it's gone…"

During gardening season, my husband and I, along with other community gardeners, spent every other weekend weeding, trimming, harvesting a little here and there and replanting what had died. In the winter, we worked together to empty the beds of annuals, cut back the perennials and plan for the next garden.

While we were away that next weekend, and I had time to think about what had happened, I was surprised to realize that I routinely spent time in the garden every day. Pulling weeds and cutting herbs for dinner was my way of making the switch from the demands of my work to the calm of my home.

I needed the garden more than it needed me, and now it was gone.

It is said that no one can steal your joy. That's just not true.

I hadn't understood how much joy I had gotten from the garden or how it had helped anchor my life. What I did understand, however, was that I needed to find a new joy that would both comfort me and carry me calmly from my life as a writer/teacher at work to my life at home as a wife, mother, and grandmother.

I haven't yet found a new joy or a stronger bridge to carry me from one role to another, but I'm working on it. Thanks for asking, but, no, I'm not rebuilding the garden. It's time to dig a little deeper, understand my own needs a little better, and become not only more aware but more responsible for my own joy…a joy that can't be so easily taken away.

You Really Want to Be an Expert? Or Do You Just Want to Have Some Fun?

My office is on a one-block street in downtown Raleigh with four office buildings on the south side of the street and two residences on the north. For the most part, it's a quiet, tucked-away location.

For the most part. But, every day of the week without fail, someone at the corner residence begins to practice the drums at 3 p.m., charging relentlessly through various drum rolls, rim shots, thumps and bumps until 4:30 p.m.. Without fail.

Windows closed at my office. Doors locked. Curtains drawn. We hear it.

Malcolm Gladwell, in his book, *Outliers: The Story of Success,* contends that 10,000 hours of practice can turn anyone into an expert.

Let's do the math. If my drummer practices 1.5 hours a day, 7 days a week, generously taking off 21 days a year for his birthday, vacations and holidays, he would put in 417.5 hours of practice a year.

At this rate, it would take him approximately 24 years to reach Gladwell's suggested 10,000 hours to become an expert percussionist. Which is a good argument to start practicing when you are young. Very young...like say three years old young.

But what if being an expert at playing the drums, or becoming an expert at anything, is overrated? What if there's more to life than becoming an expert?

How many hours would it take to get to a perfect double stroke roll? How many hours to become a competent musician?

How many hours will get you to the edge of believing you sound good? Good enough to call up a few friends and form a garage band?

Back to my quiet street. If my office were on a busy downtown thoroughfare rather than a hidden one block street, the drummer's practice sessions would easily be drowned out by the noise of cars, buses, garbage trucks and people walking by. No one would notice.

But, on my quiet block, he or she is heard and, yes, judged by those who listen to him/her day after day stumble through a drum roll, and clip rather than hit a good solid rim shot.

There are days when the drumming is just good enough to become part of the background music of working in a downtown office. Others, when the practice sessions totter on the edge of awful and people in the building complain to each other about the noise. Despite the disruption in our blessed solitude, no one has ever gone so far as to walk across the street and beg the drummer to stop.

Truth: the drummer has good and bad days, but the practicing never stops. The drummer never gives up.

I have come to appreciate the persistence of the drummer. I have no idea if he or she has ever considered the possibility of becoming an expert or going professional, or if they are working to achieve a flawless smooth drum roll, or even hold out hopes of someday being asked to join a band. But it is clear there is something very satisfying about the process because the drummer continues to practice, good day or bad, for an hour and a half every day.

Lately there are times when the practicing feels more purposeful, sometimes even playful. When this happens, I like to believe the drummer is less concerned with becoming an expert than with having a little fun. In short, I am beginning to think he practices every day because he enjoys playing the drums.

For that reason, I've come to look forward to his practice sessions. They keep my head clear about my own life goals.

Perfection pales in comparison to the joy of trying...over and over again... to get better.

If You Have the Privilege of Being Seventy, Don't Waste It!
Seventy is the new outspoken. Speak up!

Old is hot. Hot flashes. Hot ticket. Hot. Being old and hot has even made the news. In "Younger Longer: Can We Age Better? Or Even Stop the Process of Aging?" (*The New Yorker* May 20, 2019), Adam Gopnik raises an interesting question: What if modern medicine and aging research could hold the clock steady on being middle aged, thereby allowing us to get older without growing old? Think of being seventy or even eighty without worrying about climbing a flight of stairs or apologizing for "a senior moment."

On May 16, 2019, the *New York Times* published two articles in the Styles section about aging with style: "Polishing the Silver" by Ruth La Ferla and "Take That Graying Mane and Add a Burst of Fun" by Crystal Martin. Both articles made growing old and going grey sound like an invitation to a dress-up party.

I'm all for getting older with a little style in my step. For the first time in my life, thanks to the miracle of double cataract surgery, I can see well enough without glasses to artfully apply eye shadow and draw on a smooth bit of eyeliner. You better believe I intend to fancy on some makeup every day for the rest of my life. It looks great. Makes me feel a touch glamorous and, most importantly, well armored to go out into the world and have my say. You see, getting older is no longer the voice-silencing, invisibility-inducing sentence it used to be.

Seventy is about more than feeling and looking good.

Seventy is the new outspoken.

Seventy is a privilege. It's a gift. It's about time we embraced that gift and used our years of making mistakes while doing some things right to be something better, do something bigger, and live larger, as though we don't have enough time left to do anything else.

You think being seventy is hard? Try being eighteen. Can you imagine? Have you ever known such chaos? Such uncertainty? The stock market is bobbling at every tweet and tariff. Unemployment is up, then it's down. Getting a college education costs more than ever before and many are left paying off student loans for decades after graduation, making it impossible to get ahead, buy a house or start a family. There's climate change riding the winds of terrifying hurricanes, tornados and flooding rains. There are whispers of war here, there, everywhere. Senseless violence…and guns. Don't get me started.

Too much is happening for us to be silent. Those of us lucky enough to be seventy have the protection of age to speak up. It's time for us to step up to the plate, be the elders, the wise ones, the ones who have lived long enough to speak truth to power.

It's time to find new ways to "act your age."

1) Be a mentor. Find someone who can use your expertise, your help. It won't be hard. Have coffee with them. Talk. Listen. Especially listen. Offer support, direction, whatever is needed. It's that helping hand thing and it works. When was the last time you had a conversation? A real one that mattered. This is your chance.

2) Get involved with an issue. The environment. Politics. School lunches. Classroom size. Money for the arts. Guns. Voting rights. Climate change. Transportation. Health care.

Pick an issue, then do something about it. Now.

3) Find a new hobby. It doesn't matter whether it's baking cakes, planting a garden, building birdhouses or writing poems. Share what you love with someone. That's how we build stronger communities. Make new friends. Create a kinder world.

4) Take care of yourself. Exercise even if you have never exercised before. Exercise your body, and your voice. Be strong. Be focused. Raise a little hell. Have a little fun, and don't ever think for a minute that there's nothing you can do to change things.

You're seventy or maybe eighty or, hallelujah! Ninety!!

You're not old. You're one of the warriors.

All those years of living have prepared you for this chance to make a difference. Step out, step up, and speak up!

You'll be surprised who is waiting to hear what you have to say.

Want to Upscale Your Downsizing? Take Your Memories Along.

Downsizing isn't about letting go and giving up. It's about sorting through the things you have carried around and the things you love so you can live it up! It's a chance to lighten your load and focus on what carries memories for you and makes you happy. Get rid of the things that don't matter and only keep the things you love. And, while you're at it, give yourself permission to wear your grandmother's pearls and use your Sunday-best china every day. Because today is that day you've been waiting for to use your special things. You're all grown up, so go for it.

Once you downsize, step out into your new, less burdened life with a clear sense of who you have become.

When my mother-in-law realized it was time to downsize, for both her ease and her wellbeing, she hired someone to help her. I don't remember her name. Let's just call her Angel.

She came to my mother-in-law's well-appointed spacious home and spent a day talking with her about what she had done, where she had lived, and what she loved the most about her life. While they talked, Angel walked through the house with my mother-in-law, asking her about the artwork, the furniture: where each of the objects came from, and what they meant to her.

Objects matter. They are powerful. They carry memories. They harbor dreams. They are the treasured things we own that make a house our home. Angel understood this and wanted my mother-in-law to leave her well-loved home with her memories intact.

The next day, she brought a drawing of my mother-in-law's new home showing where her most loved possessions would reside. Just as carefully as Angel had listened to my mother-in-law's stories, she had translated those stories into a new setting and given them a new, uncluttered life.

When moving day came, Angel and her crew arrived early in the morning, packed my mother-in-law's most loved memories and dreams, and whisked them away to the new place, leaving everything else behind to be sold, shipped to family members, or given to charity.

By four o'clock that afternoon, my mother-in-law's furniture, along with her memories and dreams, were in place at her new apartment, and what had once been a tentative and scary step into leaving a home and starting a downsized life, had morphed into a new life in a new home filled with precious memories and dreams.

It was by all accounts, the easiest move ever.

As Angel so clearly demonstrated, there are things in our lives and our homes that take up space, and there are cherished objects filled with powerful memories that give us breath and pleasure. In short: there's a whole lot of stuff we should, and can, leave behind.

If you do it like Angel did, downsizing can become a pleasure.

So, how do you let go enough to discover what matters?

I think the hardest things to let go of are those gifts you have gotten over the years that bear the memory of the giver more than they capture your memories.

Unless you want to haul all your clutter with you, you should use downsizing as a chance to shed things that don't matter, rediscover those that do matter, and free the things you have been keeping for "special occasions" into loved objects you will enjoy every day for the rest of your life.

Downsizing is about living a good life for the rest of your life.

Make this move a pro-active and positive one.

Instead of either storing or getting rid of the good china, your best clothing, that gorgeous string of pearls that once belonged to your grandmother, the silver candlesticks, and your best linens, plan to use them.

In fact, get rid of those things that, as Marie Kondo says, don't delight. Let downsizing be your excuse to make every day special.

Use the fancy linen. Pull out the fine china. Put on the pearls. Light the beautiful candles. Live like today and every next day you have going forward is a gift. Because it is.

Prefer the everyday to the fancy and fussy? Then give the fancy away to someone who will use it, and glory in the comfortable flannel shirt of the everyday you've always cherished.

It's your choice, but however you choose to live in your downsized life, the key is choosing. Don't drag everything with you into this next phase of your life. Make the decisions you've always wanted to but were afraid to make.

Step out into your new, less burdened life with a sense of renewed purpose. You've got this, dreams and all.

Make Room for New Growth in Your Winter Garden.

There is a beautiful, but brief moment in early August when everything is in bloom and the garden feels full and fulfilled. Plenty is the word that comes to mind. There is plenty of everything: ripe tomatoes, brilliant white daisies, fat zucchini, stalwart Black-eyed Susans, and so very much sunshine that the world feels perfect.

Then comes the tipping point when vines begin to wither, flowers go to seed, and the weeds grow bigger and bolder than the hot peppers you grew to keep the bugs away. The bugs, by this time, have grown immune to your ecological attempts at keeping them at bay and have taken to eating everything you've left alone to ripen on the vine.

This tipping point is so overwhelming, and the heat so overbearing, it is easy to quietly step away from the garden and let the wildness take over.

Given enough moments of neglect, the natural passing of time, and change of the seasons, there comes, for me, the best of the gardening year: putting things to rest and preparing the winter garden.

There is something ever so satisfying about pulling up the weeds, withered vegetable plants and the dying annuals, while cutting back the perennials, and mulching in preparation for next year's garden.

The work of preparing for another year of planting is full of hope and promise. In fact, it might be my favorite gardening activity of the whole year because it is spare and beautiful in its neatness: prepared and ready for something new to happen.

In my novel, *Lillian's Garden*, the main character, Helen, has taken on the task of maintaining the garden of her mother-in-law, Lillian, long after Lillian has died. But, when Helen makes the decision to take over the garden, she continues, year after year, to recreate the garden exactly as her mother-in-law had always planted it.

The garden in the story becomes a symbol of how Helen's life has become hedged in and psychologically crippled. When, by the end of the book, she at last allows herself to plant her own garden, her life changes.

Life in the garden doesn't always have to be tomatoes and twisting out of control cucumber vines. It can be dahlias, sweet peas, and delicate cosmos.

There can be kohlrabi instead of cabbage, snapdragons instead of snap peas, and tomatillos instead of tomatoes. The possibilities, no matter how small your garden, are endless.

What is essential about preparing the winter garden is making room for new dreams and new challenges.

One of the most significant insights gleaned from the Feng Shui movement is that, like preparing your winter garden, you should clean out your bookcases every year, removing those books that no longer reflect your current life.

Think of your collection of books as a garden of thoughts. Weed out the books that no longer fit your life. Put those old ideas to rest. Make room for new ideas, and while you're sorting, find some old ideas and dreams you've long forgotten about. Dust them off. Spend some time with them and decide if they are dreams that should be nurtured and revived.

When you clear your shelves of old ideas and clean out your garden of those things that have served their purpose and are now withered, you are making room for new ideas, for change, for growing a bigger, brighter life: a better life garden.

Life is Full of Tomato Lessons.

Perfection is fleeting, especially when it comes to tomatoes. Don't believe me? Try making a fresh tomato salad in January.

I'm talking real tomatoes, perfect tomatoes. The kind that rests heavy in your hand. Something lightweight that looks like a tomato but has been plucked green in Mexico, hauled in a truck and dumped at your local grocery store is not perfection. It is a trick to make you think you can eat good tomatoes all year round.

You can't.

Tomatoes are summer. Hot weather. Sunshine. Rain. The best, so ripe and heavy, they fall into your hand when you reach out to pluck them from the vine. Their skins are tight. Deep red, saturated with color. Go organic and do not be afraid of an occasional blemish. Handle them gently. Let your thumb glide over their tight skin. There should be some give if you push a little, but no softness. Soft tomatoes are for sauce. The firm ones are for salads or a wicked indulgence of a BLT, a chilled glass of wine and a bowl of sliced peaches for dessert. Indulge yourself: this kind of wonderful only lasts a moment.

Late summer is the moment.

If you don't grow tomatoes, find a friend who has a garden and ask if you might unburden them of a tomato or two. When tomatoes reach the pinnacle of perfection, their abundance can overwhelm even the most devoted tomato gardeners. Don't have friends who grow tomatoes? Buy from a local farm market.

Purchase as many as you can carry. Sun-drenched, summer ripe tomatoes are gifts from the gods. Be kind. Share. You will be loved beyond measure for your generosity.

Years ago, we went with friends to a local restaurant and, much to our joy, discovered the bar was lined from end to end with ripening tomatoes. While we were having drinks, the owner served us a platter of grilled homemade Italian sausage presented on a bed of freshly picked and thickly sliced, homegrown tomatoes, generously salted and drizzled with olive oil.

Whatever else we ate that evening was quickly forgotten. But I will always remember those tomatoes.

A word or two about best tomato practices. Do not put them in your refrigerator. Turn them stem down and line them up on your kitchen counter. They like being at room temperature. Don't let them sit there too long and go soft from age. Eat them on sandwiches, as a side dish with scrambled eggs, or as a bed for grilled fish or meats. If they start to soften, make a fresh tomato sauce or a quick batch of gazpacho.

Always sharpen your knife before slicing into a tomato. You want to make a clean cut that doesn't mash the tomato and release all the precious juice onto your cutting board. Don't own a knife sharpener? Use a serrated breadknife. It's not ideal, but better than a dull knife and makes a cleaner cut.

My favorite summer indulgence is a fresh tomato salad. Allow one large tomato per person and adjust the other ingredients according to taste and how many tomatoes you are using. You'll want to serve this salad with a crusty French bread so you can dip the bread in the remaining juice once the salad is eaten.

Tomato Salad (Serves 6)
6 large ripe tomatoes
1-2 Tbs. of capers per layer of tomatoes; capers are salty, so adjust the amount of capers to your taste
1 medium red onion, thinly sliced and diced
A large handful of fresh basil (needs to be fresh basil)
A generous pinch of salt per each layer of tomatoes
Olive oil (1 Tbs. per layer of tomatoes if you are arranging tomatoes on a small platter...2 Tbs. per layer if you are using a large platter)
Either red wine or balsamic vinegar, your choice. For every 2 Tbs. of olive oil, use 1 Tbs. of vinegar.
Feta cheese (optional)

Slice the tomatoes and arrange the first layer, one tomato slice deep, on a platter. Sprinkle with capers, thin bits of red onion, coarsely chopped basil and salt. Dribble olive oil over the tomatoes. Arrange a second layer of tomatoes and repeat with capers, red onion, chopped basil, salt and a dribble of olive oil. Continue arranging layers until you have used up all the tomatoes and onions.

Sprinkle top layer with vinegar.

Top with feta (optional).

Cover and put the salad in the refrigerator. Chill for at least an hour to allow the vinegar to seep through the layers and mix the flavors together.

Behold, the Great Judeo-Christian Bakeoff!

When friends and family gather to share a meal at Thanksgiving, they bring more than food to the table. They bring family history and traditions, fond food memories and homage to the people they have loved and lost.

It's not just another green bean casserole. It's your Aunt Jean's Green Bean Casserole that was your dad's favorite. It's your sister's best cornmeal rolls. Your brother's mashed potatoes laced with heavy cream, butter, salt and a dash of cayenne. Your mother's turkey gravy seasoned with the pan drippings, simmered slowly and seasoned liberally with salt and pepper. When she died, you inherited the big cast iron skillet she used every year to make the gravy, and you continue to make it just like she did in a quantity that never ceases to delight your family and horrify your husband.

"Who could, or even should, eat that much gravy?" he declares every year as the massive bowl of gravy passes from hand to eager hand around the table.

So many memories, so much food! Is there any room left at your table for more traditions? More food memories? Could you possibly add one more dish to an already overflowing sideboard?

Making room at the table was the pressing issue at hand when my husband and I married. Many would call it a mixed marriage because he is Jewish and I am Christian. I like to think of it as a marriage of expanded holidays.

During our first Thanksgiving together, I discovered that his family liked to double up on the turkey dressing so they could make crispy fried croquettes (sautéed in butter) with the leftover dressing the next day to be embellished with leftover gravy. This was obviously a recipe before people began to worry about their carotid arteries and seemed outrageous in comparison to our rather innocent large stash of my mother's gravy.

Forget theology. The most shocking moments in our young marriage was when I discovered that my husband had never eaten gingerbread or mincemeat pie, and much to his horror, that I had never baked a dobos torte or eaten Mandelbrot cookies.

Thus, was born the Great Judeo-Christian Bake-Off. We invited friends to join us for drinks and dessert and took to the kitchen. Together we created gingerbread men, pumpkin pie, my mother's favorite mincemeat tarts, his mother's orange loaf and Spritzgeback cookies, his Aunt Trudel's chocolate crinkles, his Aunt Helen's lebkuchen, my sister's lemon meringue pie, almond laden Mandelbrot that are akin to biscotti but better and easier to make, and, of course, snickerdoodles and chocolate chip cookies. Then there was the debate about chocolate chip cookies being thin and crisp vs plump and chewy...my family's preference for the former, his for the latter.

When the crumbs settled on the table, the dishes were washed and put away, the winner of the day was Risa's Mother's Apple Cake: a ringer brought into the competition by a friend. This delicious fresh apple cake has since become a staple of all our family gatherings and celebrations.

The Bake-Off was a success and taught us that there will always be an infinite number of places at our table for friends, new family members and all of their delicious food memories!

Just in case you have room for one more delicious food memory on your sideboard...

Risa's Mother's Apple Cake

Pare and slice 6 medium apples. Combine with 5 Tbs. sugar and 5 tsp. cinnamon. Set aside.

Combine 3 C. all-purpose flour, 2 C. sugar, 1 Tbs. baking powder, 1 tsp. salt.

Smooth a small well in the center of flour mix, and add into the well 1 C. vegetable oil, 4 eggs lightly beaten, ¼ C. orange juice, 1 tsp. vanilla extract. Beat with wooden spoon.

Grease 9" or 10" bundt or tube pan with either butter or baker's spray (oil based)

Put in 1/3 of batter, ½ apple mix, 1/3 of batter, ½ apple mix, 1/3 of batter, spreading batter over the apples as evenly as possible for each layer.

Bake at 375°F for 1 ¼ hours or until done (inserted knife comes out clean). If cake begins to overbrown, cover top with foil.

Let sit on rack for 5-10 minutes, then loosen from pan, remove and cool on rack.

PART TWO

FIRST, LOVE YOURSELF

If You First Love Yourself, the Rest Is Easy.

Steven Norton is a good friend as well as a very successful hair stylist. Twenty-five years ago, he opened a salon in Raleigh called FLY.

It was the perfect name. That first salon was a big professional awakening for him, a kind of taking flight of his life.

Much has happened in the last 25 years. Steven developed a clientele in Raleigh, made a restless move to New York to further spread his wings, then returned to Raleigh to reopen FLY and start over. Fresh.

Recently, as his clientele has grown and he has built a thriving solo salon practice, he had an epiphany. FLY, as an acronym, could, and maybe should, stand for First Love Yourself.

He stepped back, in his words, "got off the hamster wheel", and took the time he needed to consider how he wanted to love himself.

Not surprisingly, one of the first steps he took in loving himself was to redesign his workspace. He painted the walls of his salon a clean, soft white. He bought new furniture that would hide all the clutter in his workspace. And he created a comfortable sitting area where clients could relax while waiting to have their hair colored or cut.

He's the happiest I've ever known him to be.

Steven is a skilled stylist, but more importantly, he believes that getting a haircut is a moment for his clients to step away from all the noisy chatter and busy chaos in life and have a moment of rejuvenation.

First Love Yourself.

A fresh haircut makes you look better.

Can you be better too?

Every social media toot of "do these five things and lose five pounds before your birthday," each Instagram of the perfect day/meal/vacation, and Pinterest bulletin telling you how easy it would be to retile your bathroom, use your wedding gown to make café curtains for your first home, or that niggling list of what you should or should not wear now that you are 40, 50, 60, or 70 is like having someone poke you in the eye.

I won't take those tests and I refuse to follow Facebook advice. I think the most damning advice from social media are all those posts telling women how to act and dress their age. How come they never tell men?

There's a post going around the Internet that lists a dozen or so things women shouldn't do or wear once they reach a certain age. High on that list is the notion that older women shouldn't wear eyeliner.

Until I had double cataract surgery a couple of years ago, I couldn't see well enough without my glasses to apply any kind of eye makeup.

I can now, and you better believe I plan to wear eyeliner every day for the rest of my life. I'm even considering having eyeliner written into my final directives. My favorite color eyeliner right now: teal.

When the crew came to repaint Steven's salon, they kept asking if he was going for a minimalist look with the white walls, white ceilings, white trim, and white window treatment.

White, even in various subtle shades of snow white to polar bear white, does have a minimalist feel to it, but that's not why Steven had it painted that way.

What he wanted was fresh. Uncluttered. Calm. Welcoming.

He's made it work. And he loves it.

Therein lies the magic of first loving yourself.

Once you get off the hamster wheel, shut out the chatter, quit listening to everyone else and get quiet enough to hear yourself, you can rediscover what you love about yourself.

If you were to be so bold as to rebrand your life, what color would you paint your walls?

What would you do to love yourself?

You know what they always tell you when you board a plane to go from here to there: Put on your own oxygen mask first.

Love yourself so you can have the space and energy to love someone else.

How's Your Inner Frankenstein Doing?

In 1814, Mary Shelley traveled throughout the Rhine region of Germany with Lord Byron and her lover and future husband, Percy B. Shelley. At some point in their journey, the three of them decided to have a competition to see who could write the best horror story.

Mary Shelley won.

Mary Shelley's idea of having Dr. Frankenstein use modern science to piece together a new living creature and gain immortal fame has become the fodder for numerous movies and science fiction knockoffs for more than 200 years.

It's a fascinating concept. What if you could take a body from this person, a head from another, a brain from another and, voilà, create something bigger and stronger than the sum of their parts?

As we know from the ending of the story, the results were not exactly ideal.

There's a similar kind of magical thinking in the story of The Wizard of Oz: If I only had a heart; if I only had a brain; if I only had courage.

That's the story of our lives, isn't it? If I only had _____.

Go ahead, fill in the blank. You know at some point in your life you've wished for something about yourself to be different. You believed in your heart that if you could only change some feature about how you looked or lived, it would change your life and make you taller, smarter, richer, more successful, more beautiful, your house would always be tidy, and the meals you served perfect and loved by everyone.

What is that thing for you?

Whenever I let my mind drift down Frankenstein Lane, I try to laugh it off and couch it in the framework of, "In my next life I want to have _____."

Top of my list: longer, thinner legs. Okay, and maybe one smashingly successful book that ends in a movie contract (the book publishing business these days is brutal). When my first big royalty check comes rolling in, I'll cash that sucker and buy a beach house.

When dark days hit, and they do for everyone, no matter how tall, thin, rich or successful, and the "if I had this or that or if I could change this or that about myself" thoughts come bubbling up, you need to pay attention.

When the darkness hits, it's probably time to stop what you're doing and assess where you're going and what you really want to do with your life. Truth is, you don't really need a beach house in order to regroup. For that matter, you don't have to go far away, or for long, in order to take a break and refuel; you just need to go somewhere by yourself to take a deep breath and refocus.

What did you write in that blank: If I only had _____. Do you really need that missing something in order to be smarter, taller, or happier? Or is it time to step back and discover if you already have what you need?

Maybe you don't, but maybe you do.

Mary Shelley's tale of Dr. Frankenstein lives on 200 years after it was first published because it really is a book about soul searching, about looking for some great success, some incredible scientific breakthrough, only to discover it isn't what you thought it was going to be.

It's a great read, a doorway into a chance to really think about what you would do if you used some magic powers to create a new life, and instead, created a monster.

Reading Frankenstein gives you a chance to discover, as do Dorothy and her companions in the Wizard of Oz, that you may already have what you need to find your way home to loving yourself just the way you are, short, stocky legs and all.

However, I'd still like to have one smashing book success and a movie deal.

Wouldn't we all?

Out of the Political Fantasy of *The West Wing* and into the Beautiful World of the Fab 5.

The Fab 5 say you are beautiful, and you are enough. It's time to believe them.

In 2010, a neighbor lent us season three of *The West Wing*. Our daughter had come home from college to recuperate from mono and we were looking for entertainment.

Beyond the evening news, we rarely watched television and had never seen *The West Wing*. Two episodes in, we were hooked.

Our daughter recovered, returned to school, and I found a source online that would sell me all seven seasons in a gift box.

Confession: From the first episode in season one to the very last in season seven, our family watched all 156 episodes, more than once. Okay, four times.

My friend Ingrid recently told me she has once again started watching *The West Wing*. That she needs it right now.

I understood what she meant. Watching Jed Bartlet and his crew tackle the problems of the world was like looking into a magical political mirror of what could be.

My husband has recently drawn a line in the sand: no more *West Wing*.

I don't need his approval for what to watch on television. However, now that the DVD player is gone and we live by Netflix, I haven't got a clue—nor do I care to figure out—what to do with the two remotes and the occasional interruption of the Internet. Plus, I like sitting on the couch at the end of the day watching just about anything with him. The world of the remotes is his to command, almost.

Enter the *Queer Eye's* "Fab 5."

Queer Eye was a bit of a hard sell for him until the third month of sheltering at home when we were out of things to watch. In desperation, I suggested we try the Fab 5, and we previewed the first episode.

Sold.

It isn't feel-good politics. It's feel-really-good about yourself and the world. It is a place where kindness and acceptance reign. It is a magical mirror where our diverse world cares about each other. Where people get supported and things get fixed.

If, like me, you have come to the party a beat too late, don't panic. Netflix has all five seasons waiting for you, along with a side trip to Japan.

We like to save watching *Queer Eye* for the end of the day and dole out the episodes one at a time … unless it has been a particularly horrifying news day and we need to watch two episodes.

It wasn't long after we started watching the Fab 5 when I began to dream up dozens of reasons the Fab 5 should come to our area, maybe even our home.

We don't really need Bobby Berk to paint our kitchen cabinets and re-model/renovate our living space. We have a nice home.

As for my hair, I have good hair and a terrific stylist. But you have to admit, it would be like waking up on Christmas morning to spend an afternoon with Jonathan Van Ness. Maybe go skating with him.

My husband is a wonderful baker and I'm a good cook (in fact, spent a big chunk of my professional life writing about food) so, although we don't need help in the kitchen, it would be fun hanging out with Antoni Porowski, cooking dinner for the crew.

As for our wardrobes, Tan France is welcome to rummage through our closets throwing out things from our pasts that need to go. I love the way he cuts to the chase and helps people find their new bold beautiful lives.

We could all use a little more style. In fact, last night, after the seventh episode in season four, my husband remarked that maybe his pants could be tailored a little slimmer. We are both experimenting with the French tuck, sometimes more successfully than others.

And who wouldn't want to have a chance to sit and talk with Karamo Brown? I mean, really.

The Fab 5 calls the people they help heroes.

That's it, isn't it? We all need to believe we are here to have a good life and to also make the world better. To be heroes.

However, heroes need to believe in themselves. They need to reach deep and discover their real beauty. Their hidden power of self-confidence.

Whenever Jonathan finishes the cut and style and leans into the mirror and says, "Honey, just look at that beautiful face … you are gor-geous," we want to see ourselves in that mirror and believe it.

Who Cares About the Color of Your Parachute, What Color Is Your Hair?

I recently made an appointment to apply for the new "Real ID", i.e., a driver's license meant to establish my true identity better than my old driver's license could, that will soon be required for boarding domestic flights and other such identity situations. Appointment verification and documents in hand, I cut to the front of the line.

I should note here that the line of DMV customers without appointments snaked out of the office, through the corridor and down the block.

I had heard a number of horror stories regarding the careful scrutiny of the various documents required by DMV for the new licenses: a recent utility bill from your current address complete with your name, or some other bill that would confirm your name and your address (not your spouse's or your roommate's), a social security card, birth certificate, and a photo ID complete with your full legal name and date of birth (i.e., a passport), and went well prepared.

As usual, I was pressed for time, hence the appointment, and came fully armed with a folder of required documents and a few backups just in case they didn't like what I was presenting. In short, I had my scheduled appointment and my ducks in a row. I was ready to go.

When it was my turn, I stepped up and presented my documents. The clerk picked through my offerings, chose a few, copied them, and then asked for my current driver's license.

"Is the address correct?" she asked.

"Yes." I have learned over time that when conducting official business, short answers are best.

"Do you still want to be an organ donor?"

"Yes."

"Is all the other information on your license correct?"

"Yes."

She typed for a few minutes then spoke again.

"Please look at the screen and verify the information I've typed for your new license."

I looked. It seemed fine.

"It's correct," I responded, gathering my documents.

"Are you sure?"

I looked again and nodded my head. Everything seemed in order.

She hesitated then said: "Your present license says that you have brown hair. Do you want me to say you have brown hair?"

"Sure," I replied, glancing back at the long line of folks waiting their turn to present their documents.

The clerk didn't seem to be in a hurry.

"Your new license will be good until 2022. Do you still want me to say your hair is brown? Let me take your picture."

She instructed me to look at the light above the screen. The light blinked. My picture came up on her computer. She turned it around so I could see.

On inspecting my picture, it appeared that whatever brown hair I once had was now a whisper of soft brown, speckled with grey. Lots of grey. It was not some noble or respectable salt and pepper blend, but rather a few soft brown hairs scattered amongst a sea of unmistakable grey.

"Grey?" I asked.

"Good choice," she said, making the correction.

When I got to my car, I called my daughter so I could talk to my three-year-old granddaughter.

"What color is GaGa's hair?" I asked. Lily is a total devotee of Crayola Crayons and takes great pride in knowing her colors.

"Silver," Lily said without hesitation.

"Grey?" I prompted.

"No, silver."

I looked at my reflection in the rearview mirror. My hair looked more like a patch of neglected tarnished silver rather than something shiny and new.

Funny how life can sneak up on you.

At my next haircut, I hesitated for a moment before broaching the subject, but asked anyway.

"What color is my hair?"

Steven, both friend and stylist, took a moment to brush his fingers through my hair thoughtfully from side to side.

"Sable," he said. "Your hair is definitely sable colored."

I'm a bit unsure about the exact color of sable, but it sounded rich. Luxurious. Silky. I loved the idea my hair had gone sable rather than grey and loved him for saying it!

It Might be Time to Quit Waiting for That Special Day to Arrive.

Our eldest son and his wife recently gave me a beautiful leather handbag for my birthday. Red. A seriously bright, shouting red that could easily be mistaken for orange in the sunshine, but could never be mistaken for boring.

It was, and is, perfect. It's small but big enough for my wallet, sunglasses, passport, and car keys. In fact, it is the perfect size to keep me organized. It has an extra-long cross-body strap, which fits nicely over a dress coat and hugs comfortably at my hip when I'm walking around in jeans and a t-shirt.

It is a love-at-first-sight kind of handbag.

When I opened the present, my husband's first reaction was: "Nice, you should save it for a special occasion."

No, no, and no.

You see, I've recently said goodbye to too many friends. I have baked more than my share of casseroles to soothe broken hips, simmered too many soup pots of homemade cinnamon applesauce to tamp down nausea from chemotherapy, and written way too many condolence cards to believe that there is some special day out there just waiting for me to unearth my beautiful, red leather purse and use it.

Today is a good day. Tomorrow is great. The day after that, if I get to live it, is a gift I can't afford to waste.

Would that I will live long enough to wear out my red leather purse, and if I do, I will go out and buy a new one.

Which takes me to velvet, and why I recently decided to throw away the idea of buying yet another sensible, all-purpose cotton shirt or black sweater that would go with everything. Instead, I bought a deep plum velvet tunic for myself. I like velvet. It can be rolled up and packed without getting wrinkled. It's soft, flows nicely, looks special, and you can throw it in the washing machine and dryer. What's not to like about it? I even think it pairs well with jeans.

It's also bold. Feels all dressed up and ready for a party.

That's my wish: to go boldly into the world for the rest of my life, ready to celebrate another day. Any day. In fact, every day with my beautiful red purse in tow.

Who Writes the Fashion Rules? Better Yet, Why Do We Care?

I first got schooled regarding fashion when I was in second grade. On that fateful morning, I had chosen to wear a red plaid skirt paired with my favorite bright pink sweater.

At the ripe old age of six I was not only allowed to dress myself but could walk the two blocks to school on my own. When I crossed the street to the second block, a third grader, who was an only child and had both a fine wardrobe and a divine sense of her personal fashion acumen, bounced down her front steps in her polished black and white saddle oxfords, hands on hips, to tell me, with certainty and righteousness in her voice, that one should NEVER wear pink and red together.

She was wearing a grey flannel circular poodle skirt and a white blouse topped with a creamy white cardigan adorned with pearl buttons.

Funny what memories get stuck in your head.

I remember that skirt because I wanted one. Wanted, but never got one. They were the height of elementary school fashion that year and way beyond what my mother thought we should spend money on. I was also pretty keen on owning a cardigan sweater with pearl buttons. Never got one of those either.

My mother didn't believe in fashion or fads or spending a lot of money on clothes. She believed in things that could be laundered in the washing machine. She didn't go for fancy flannel this or that, satin, silk, lace, or heaven forbid...velvet! She liked simple things like cotton, the sale rack at the local department store, and serviceable clothing that could be worn to school as well as church on Sundays. She also liked skirts and dresses that had deep hems she could let down midway through the year so they would last from the first day of school to summer vacation.

Practical was her clothing mantra.

What I most remember about that red plaid/pink sweater morning was the shame I felt that I didn't know the rules about what one should or should not wear. I was also startled to discover that, in fact, there were rules about what one should or should not wear.

Next came the hardcore shocking discovery that one shouldn't wear a white dress until Easter and never after Labor Day.

The "no white" rule until Easter kept my head spinning for years. I had no idea colors were so socially and religiously charged.

Things were sailing along fine in my limited knowledge of fashion rules until folks in college began talking about being an "autumn" or "summer" and what the various "seasons" should wear to look their best.

No matter how many *Cosmopolitan* beauty quizzes I took during this new fashion twist of fate, I never could figure out my season. The only thing I knew for sure was that I was Scotch-Irish, sunburned easily, and should probably always wear a hat or at least sunscreen.

Then along came Lily.

Lily is our granddaughter. Lily has dressed herself since she could walk. She is fierce in her determination and fashion choices.

On one particularly wild day of getting dressed, our daughter made the mistake of suggesting that perhaps Lily had not made good choices and might want to tone it down a tick or two.

Lily's retort: "There are no rules about what to wear."

She inspires me.

I dress up more since Lily has arrived in my life. I'm also bolder in my choices.

Just yesterday, in a moment of feeling rather shopworn and February dreary, I reached deep into my closet, found my white jeans, paired them with a royal blue velvet top (that some might think should only be worn to a New Year's Eve party) added a favorite silk scarf and went to work.

No rules. I like that.

Thanks, Lily.

What Would Frances McDormand Do?

Call me old fashioned. I not only own an iron, but I also own an ironing board, and I have been known to iron my clothes.

Okay, that's an exaggeration. I rarely iron. But, I do have an iron and an ironing board, and I am presently struggling with whether or not to be rumpled, cool, and comfortable rather than crisply ironed and professional looking in a time of global warming.

I am originally from the North and lived for many years in the bliss of silk. I love silk. While living and working in Chicago, I amassed a fortune in slightly oversized fluid silk blouses that wanted nothing better than to hang comfortably from my shoulders as though I were born to flutter through life, wrinkles and all!

On the advice of a fashion designer I knew, I never ironed my silk shirts. Rather, I washed them by hand then tossed them into the dryer with tennis balls. Straight from the dryer without a hint of smoothness, they made me look like I was competent and comfortable enough with myself at thirty to not give a flip about a wrinkle or two.

Then I moved with my husband to North Carolina and discovered that humidity and heat rise together and saturate the air to the point where water simply falls to the ground in droplets. Tourists call it rain. I call it Southern tears.

FYI, it's hard not to sweat in the South, and, when sweat meets silk, the fabric sticks to your body like a wet sail in a storm.

Within a year or two of moving to North Carolina, one by one, my beautiful silk blouses got pushed to the back of the closet in the hope of the long dry winter that never seemed to materialize. Then came hot flashes and the end of silk in my life.

That's when I discovered linen. Cool on a hot day, dreamy looking in the catalogues and on store racks, so very wrinkled by ten o'clock in the morning.

For the first couple of years, I sent my linen shirts and dresses out to be laundered, lightly starched and pressed: smooth and beautiful. That bit of momentary elegance cost me a fool's fortune. By the time I walked from our house to my car and buckled my seatbelt, my put-together look invariably wadded up on me.

Then one morning it came to me. If there was no way to stop linen from wrinkling, why not treat it like fine silk and flaunt its inherent imperfections?

I boldly threw my linen shirts into the washing machine, took them out, gave them a quick snap to chase a few wrinkles away, and hung them up to dry. However, every time I put on one of my laundered but not ironed linen shirts, I looked so rumpled I didn't have the courage to leave the house, not to mention go to work. Like my silk blouses, the linen got pushed to the back of the closet.

Age brings wisdom, or so we hope.

A couple of weeks ago, I gave two of my long-ignored linen shirts to a daring woman entrepreneur I know. What did she do? She washed them, gave them a good shake, hung them up to dry then put them on wrinkles and all and took command of a board meeting.

She's so self-confident, I'm not even sure she owns an iron.

It was then that I had to stop and ask myself: Would Frances McDormand care if her linen shirt got a little wrinkled on the movie set?

Life is a hot flash.

Like Frances McDormand, I have earned my grey hair, along with the fine lines and wrinkles on my face and neck, and I'm kind of proud I got here.

Which is why I decided it is high time that I embrace my wrinkled linen blouses and dresses, not just as clothing but as badges of honor for having made it to my badass years.

A Moment of Sanity Brought to You by Hygge.

My mother didn't have a drop of Scandinavian blood in her and for sure had never ever heard the word hygge, but she often served dinner by candlelight.

I'm not talking about special occasion, fancy china kind of dinners, but Kraft mac and cheese with green beans and a salad, canned tomato soup and grilled cheese sandwiches, or chicken pot pies straight from the grocery store freezer to our table.

These simple candlelight meals often hinted that our father had been away just a beat too long on a business trip. In short, it had been a hard day and we were leaning on our mother's last raw nerve.

Candlelight meant that we should sit still, be quiet, and eat in a civilized manner. Calm was called for, and we had better manage to get through the meal without a fight or a cross word or we would be sent to our rooms indefinitely, or at least until we were old enough to move out and fend for ourselves.

It was a warning.

These candlelit dinners were my favorite meals — paper napkins, everyday dishes, canned green beans and all — because they were everything we needed to get through another day with some grace.

When my husband and I had children, I broke out the candles. Not just on unraveled nerve nights but most nights because I remembered those candlelit meals and knew our children deserved a moment of calm at the end of the day as well as we did.

Enter hygge: a way to calm the day and celebrate the moment.

We were introduced to the concept of hygge (pronounced hue-guh) late in 2019 by dear friends from Copenhagen. They had been living in our building while working on a project in the US and had joined a group of us who regularly shared meals together. They were getting ready to return to Denmark, and we had gathered in their home for a shared meal and an evening learning about hygge.

Everyone brought a dish to share and dressed up for the occasion. We were sad our friends would soon be leaving but happy to have one more meal together.

The evening was illuminated by dozens of candles. Drinks were served. There was lots of talk, laughter and good food. It was relaxing and soothing in the way spending time with good friends can be.

Hygge, beyond lighting candles and slowing down the pace of the day, is something you do for yourself to enjoy life in the moment.

Our friends left for Denmark, and before any of us really understood what living through a pandemic was going to demand of us, we were knee-deep in anxiety, not knowing what was going to happen next. We never knew for sure what had hit us, never had a chance to catch our breath, and never could figure out or count on what was going to happen next.

In truth, we are still wondering when it will be safe to take our masks off, if our jobs will be secure, our community intact, and our children prepared to go back out into the world.

It's been scary. Unsettling. Challenging. Isolating.

We have had to fashion nooks and crannies in our homes into little office spaces and homeschool corners. We've fallen into a domestic routine that is unlike any other we have known. Home has been where we are, with just our immediate family 24/7. We've had to make peace and space with living together. Meals…well…meals…three of them, day in and day out.

Here's my takeaway: When you aren't exactly sure if we've rounded the corner on a week and are sitting squarely once again on a weekend, you might want to do something to change the pace.

When, during COVID, I couldn't figure out if it was Wednesday or Saturday, I decided it was time to pull out the candles again. Ones I have been saving for holiday meals, ones my mother-in-law gave me 15 years ago when she downsized, a few handmade ones purchased at art shows, and two boxes of votives in case the lights go out.

We now eat lunch as well as dinner by candlelight. We talk more softly once the candles are lit. Linger longer at the table as the candles burn down.

It's a little bit of hygge that reminds us it is okay to do something nice for ourselves and enjoy a kinder, calmer moment of life.

It's something we are planning to continue after the masks come off and we feel like we are living in a normal day again.

Who Needs the Grinch? Alzheimer's Stole My Christmas!

It didn't start in 1985, but that was the Christmas that made us stop and acknowledge that our mother's memory loss, her changed personality and her growing irrational behavior were too pronounced for us to continue to pretend that she was just having another bad day.

She was confused. Wasn't sure who was showing up for dinner or exactly why we were all there. Then, after we opened presents and made dinner, she moved her artificial tree into the corner of the basement and covered it with a sheet. When I offered to help her take off the ornaments and put everything away, she said she was too tired to deal with it. When I pushed, she got annoyed and told me that she never took down the tree, but instead, just kept it covered and stored in the corner for the next year.

It was a strange wake-up call. The tree and all its trappings were a special ritual in our family. When we were children, putting up the tree meant drinking eggnog and eating peppermint candy canes, while we strung lights and delighted with each unwrapped bauble we were allowed to hang on the tree: plastic ones when we were little, the delicate blown glass ones as we grew older and could reach the higher branches. Our mother, of course, always settled the angel in place at the top of the tree.

Like a wrecking ball, Alzheimer's swung high and mighty through the next fifteen years of Christmas, and our family continued, year after year, to visit mom and do our best to connect and create a celebration.

One year, as we were preparing to book plane tickets, our children staged a small revolt. They didn't want to fly. They felt it was too hard to go so fast from here to there.

I understood. They loved her, but found it jolting to go from their lives to hers in one short flight.

That's when we started taking the 11-hour train ride from Raleigh to Michigan. It was the best way to comfortably travel from here to there, sitting in the observation car watching the holiday lights pass by as the train wound its way through small towns and backyards to Christmas.

Five years later, when we moved Mom into the Alzheimer's wing of the Chelsea Methodist Home, my sister and I took down her Christmas tree, dividing the ornaments into various boxes to share with our two brothers. My box is in our storage room. Although I continue to love buying gifts and making a special Christmas dinner for friends and family, I long ago quit putting up a tree, because as Alzheimer's took over and our mother declined, the holiday and all its glitter got sideswiped.

Which brings me to a very satisfying moment when I decided to go for it and burn down Christmas.

A couple of years ago, my husband, who loves a party, offered our home for our condominium's holiday open house. While he merrily baked goodies, I went to a secondhand store looking for someone else's Christmas memories to adorn our home. That's when I found an entire village of fancy candles: churches, schools, snow covered shops, pine trees, a Santa Claus and a snowman. All too precious and pretty to burn.

I bought all of them, put aluminum foil over our buffet, sprayed it with fake snow and planted a Christmas candle village. I even assembled a Lego fire truck complete with fireman and set him up by one of the houses.

When the first guest came through the door, I poured myself a glass of wine and lit the candles one-by-one.

It was a cathartic moment. Our guests loved it!

At the end of the evening when the candles at last burned out, I let go of all those dark Christmases and made a promise to go forward building new memories for myself and my family, ones that will last, I hope, beyond my lifetime.

How to Enrich Your Life by Sitting Still and Daydreaming.
Are you willing to test your daydreaming skills?

Schedule a meeting with a friend. Coffee, lunch, or an after-work drink. Your pick. Ease into this. Trust me. It's going to be hard. Harder than you think.

First, arrange to arrive five minutes early for your meeting. Now, try sitting still while you wait. Really still. The kind of still where your mind is forced to wander or just to rest easy for a moment.

How hard can being alone and sitting still for five minutes be?

Very hard. Here's the catch. You cannot grab your phone to check your messages. You can't pull your laptop from your bag and boot it up. In fact, if your phone rings, you can't answer it.

The point is to just sit there. Be still. Let your mind go. Look out the window. If you feel like it, you can smile at someone passing by. If someone you know walks by, do that thing with your head that says hello, but you don't have time to talk.

Do not dig in your purse for anything, not even a stick of gum, or search for something to read.

Just sit there. Still. Really still.

Have you looked at your watch? I bet you have.

Do the five-minute trial a couple of times until you no longer feel antsy and ready to jump out of your skin at four minutes, because you haven't checked your phone for messages or tapped on your weather app.

Here's the next step. The real test. Try for 10 minutes.

The first time I did 10 minutes, at minute seven, in desperation, I reached into my purse, pulled out a scrap of paper, and started taking notes... for this article.

My goal is to be able to sit still for 15 minutes. Fifteen minutes waiting. Sitting. Thinking. Looking out the window. Hands like resting birds in my lap. No phone to grab my attention away from the moment. No scrap of paper hastily drawn from my purse like some life preserver that might keep me from drowning in the unconnected silence of it all.

It's a goal worth achieving. One I'm itching to take on.

Being able to sit still won't necessarily make me a better person. But it might help quiet my mind. Might smooth the jagged edge of the chaos swirling in the world around me. Might make it possible for me to notice how tree roots seem to like resting half in and half out of the Earth, or how the clouds change shape as they slip across the sky.

Here's why I'm doing this. I want to recapture what it used to feel like when there was no cell phone in my life. No email begging for my attention. I want to feel like I once did when I wasn't tethered so tightly to the world and, therefore, was able to have my own thoughts, my own ideas, not just a constant reflex reaction to everything happening in the world.

I'd like to get back there because I think I lost something along the connected highway we're traveling together. I'd like to know what it feels like again to be still. To take a deep breath. To wait. Patiently.

I miss being patient. I miss what it feels like to anticipate. To wait. To let my mind be unfettered without an agenda or connected destination. I miss daydreaming.

Remember daydreaming? Those little escapes where your mind felt free? I got in trouble more than once in school for daydreaming. My teachers told my parents my mind wandered. That I didn't always pay attention in class. That I was a dreamer.

I want to be a dreamer again.

It's going to be hard, but I think it's worth a try. I'm up to 10 minutes now. And anxiously anticipating the day when I can sit still for 15 whole minutes by myself and daydream.

Let me know how you do.

Got Retirement Plans?

Here's the truth. Some are better at retirement than others.

Take my husband, for instance. He's a total pro. He didn't take phased retirement like most of his colleagues at the university. He went cold turkey. 100%. Didn't look back.

Once retired, he began playing the violin again, something he hadn't done regularly since college. He started taking lessons. He practices every day. A good first step.

Next, he decided he wanted to learn something about art, so he enrolled in art history classes. By the end of this semester, he will have exhausted almost every art history course offered at the university.

He's a five-year retirement veteran and offers to go to lunch with any and everyone who is contemplating retiring. He tells friends that he likes being retired. Has no regrets but understands that it's not for everyone.

I'm happy for him. He's even started baking bread this last year, which is nice for us. He also bakes cakes for friends and family for any, and all occasions. He'd even bake a cake for me if I ever announced my retirement.

My retirement. I'm trying to come to grips with the idea, but I'm not any good at it.

When my husband retired, I decided to give it a try. I approached my potential retirement as kind of like a soft opening for a new restaurant.

I've been a freelance writer for more than 50 years, so I don't exactly have to hand in paperwork in order to announce my retirement. Nor do I need to meet with the HR department to discuss how I want to take the payout on my 401K. So, deciding I'm retiring doesn't carry as much fanfare as it might for someone who has had, as my mother used to remind me, "a real job."

It's complicated.

My first phase of retirement seemed simple enough. I have an office downtown and for the most part, I'm a long-standing 9-5/M-F kind of writer. It's my job. I also teach some, lecture some, and write a wide variety of things, including this column.

In what I thought was a bold move, I gave myself permission to attend a water aerobics exercise class at the local pool M/W/F from 8:30-9:30, which gets me into the office all showered and ready to go for the day by 10 a.m. rather than my usual 9.

Not bad, I thought, for a first try at retirement. Except, the day wasn't long enough, so I wound up having to shift my regular 9-5 workload to 10-6.

So much for phased retirement.

Today, however, marks the beginning of my boldest move yet. I'm adding a Tues/Thurs shallow-water Pilates class that runs from 10-11, which will get me showered, changed and into the office a little before 11:30.

Here's the new plan: get up at my usual time (old habits are hard to break), eat a leisurely breakfast, read the newspaper (we still get a real copy of the *New York Times* delivered to our front door every morning…I like paper), get a jump on the day by answering a few emails from home, suit up for the pool, exercise, then go to the office.

Why take another water aerobics class?

Simple. I don't have a pocket in my swimsuit for my cell phone.

Retiring is going to require unplugging on some very basic level. Work is addictive. I realized early on that if I was going to succeed, I would have to approach my retirement one baby step at a time.

As my next birthday rolls around, I am actively exploring other phased-retirement options: taking lunch everyday away from the office and leaving the office before five at least one day a week. Baby steps. Here's one of my bolder moves: I have quit working on Federal holidays.

That last one, not working on Federal holidays, is a tough one for me. I relish the quiet days downtown when everyone else is gone. I get a lot of writing done on Federal holidays.

I'm old enough to retire. But the emotional truth is that I like writing. I like being a writer and thinking like a writer and am unsure what my life would be like if I quit being a writer. And did, what?

There's only so much time you can spend treading water before you need to get out of the pool and do something else, like take a shower and get to work.

I'm trying.

PART THREE

LESSONS FROM COVID

DieForTheDow? It's time to start sorting out what matters in life and why.

Hello, my name is Carrie, and I'm high-risk.

Right now, like many high-risk individuals, both young and old, I'm concerned about COVID-19 and will continue to be cautious even as we move to some kind of new only-wear -masks-in-crowded-buildings normal, whatever and whenever that will be.

I have two strikes against me.

Strike one: I have one kidney; the other kidney took a weird left turn a couple of years ago, collapsed, and had to be removed.

Strike two: I'm 70+ years old.

I exercise daily, I eat well, and I still work. My doctor tells me I'm in surprisingly good health. But I'm still high-risk. So is anyone with chronic asthma, heart disease, diabetes, suppressed immunity, you name it.

Anything that could compromise your wellness makes you high-risk. Smoking or heavy vaping use can put you at risk. Life is risky.

Think about that. It's not just the old who are at risk for any number of diseases or circumstances. It's a whole spectrum of young and old if they are at all compromised.

It's not just me. It could be you.

I don't know about you, but for the record, I'm not willing, like Texas Lt. Governor Dan Patrick suggested, to die in order to save the economy and keep my grandchildren from going through a Depression.

I was, however, willing to quarantine myself to be sure I neither got COVID nor gave it to anyone else. Including you. I was also willing to get vaccinated in order to protect myself and make it possible for my extended family to be safe, and for the community I live in to get back to working at the office, eating in restaurants, shopping local rather than online, you know…a normal way of living we used to embrace.

Here's my take on grandchildren. Young children need to have as many adults as possible in their lives who love them unconditionally. Grandchildren need grandparents.

Plus, grandparents, i.e., the elders of this world, are grounded in wisdom and experience. When things are coming off the rails, a little wisdom can go a long, long way—in addition to that unconditional love thing.

Here's the truth with a capital Texas T. The suggestion to push people back to work and let the old folks die in order to save the economy may have had more to do with some individuals' personal stock portfolios than it did with saving the world for the future.

Many of the people who argued that it was time to get people back to work said they wanted folks out of their homes and back in their offices to protect the economy for their grandchildren. Really?

Because their grandchildren weren't smart enough to make their own money? Or maybe investment-focused folks believed their own children were a little too reckless buying lattes and therefore weren't likely to leave anything behind for the next generation.

Maybe.

Let's talk about the stock market for a minute.

Did COVID 19 kill it? Or was it nervous investors selling off stocks that put the life of the Dow in danger?

Stock markets go down when there are large sell-offs. Sell-offs happen when people get scared that they are going to lose their investments. Investments crumble when people sell.

See how that works?

If you want the stock market, and therefore, the economy to stay afloat, don't rock the boat.

Unless you need the money to pay for food, your rent/mortgage and utility bills, don't sell your stocks. Watching the stock market tumble can be a panic-inducing thing. Don't panic.

Here's what we know about today's market economy.

1. What happened during COVID was different from what happened with the market fall in 2008.

2. We don't know for certain if the worst is behind us either economically or personally. It's unclear whether we might be headed for another pandemic and an even more unstable time.

3. The market may be lower tomorrow.

4. Historically, markets drop, but they eventually rebound.

It's important to hold tight for the rebound. Don't react to every news story. Look at your own story. If you really need the money to pay your bills, then sell only what you need to cover your expenses. Sit tight on the rest. If you're young, you have time to weather this bump and realize an economic recovery in your portfolio's value that, if you want, can be passed on to your children and grandchildren.

What helped stabilize the economy was wearing a mask, staying home, and getting vaccinated. Those were the things that slowed the spread of COVID and got people working again.

One important lesson from COVID is that you may not be compromised, but someone you pass on the street could very well be. Don't be responsible for their illness. The more people who get sick, the longer a pandemic will wreak havoc with our lives.

Call your grandparents.

Tell them you love them and hope they'll stay healthy and be around for a long, long time.

They love you. Unconditionally. And that's worth a million dollars.

What Do You Do When Yesterday, Today, and Tomorrow Become Only Now?

The first time I saw a Yesterday, Today, and Tomorrow shrub, or *Brunfelsia latifolia*, I was dazzled.

It seemed to have everything, a beautiful fragrant form and flat, two-inch flowers that not only bloomed in abundance, but magically changed colors.

Each of the flowers on the Yesterday, Today, and Tomorrow plant lasts for three days. On the first day, the bloom is deep purple; the second day the bloom turns a pastel lavender; and on the third, a creamy white.

In any given moment, from early spring through October, these plants are covered with hundreds of deep purple, pale lavender, and white blossoms creating an extravagant bouquet. Although individual blossoms are constantly blooming, changing, then dying, there are always new blossoms opening and promising to change.

Change. That's the key to its beauty.

When I first encountered this extravagant flowering shrub, I thought about how things change as we move from the past, to the present, and wonder about the future.

All seductive and beautiful things should come with a warning, and the *brunfelsia latifolia* is no exception. The plant is part of the nightshade family and contains poisonous alkaloids. The seeds from the flowers are poisonous. In addition, the beautiful berries are especially toxic.

There's a lesson there.

And, here we are, caught in the now of life in the middle of a pandemic.

Today might be the first day for some being quarantined. For others, it's their second, third, or fourth day. Some are even two-week veterans.

Everyone on the Internet is talking about the new normal.

Ask anyone who has experienced a personal loss, and they will tell you that the new normal is a big pill to swallow. There's only yesterday to lean on. Today is a tough row to hoe, and tomorrow looms like a terrifying dark cavern.

I love that so many museums, theatre venues, educational resources, and just plain fun entertaining things like taking a virtual tour through the various

National Parks have become available in an Internet outpouring of things to watch and do.

It's not as easy as some might imagine, pushing our life of busyness aside and leaning into the luxury of doing nothing and having just the moment.

Wait, is that really the way we are supposed to embrace living in the now, the new normal? Whatever that is?

Here's the thing. I can't tell you what to do or how to spend your time being quarantined and neither can anyone else.

That's the lesson of living in the now. It's only about you.

I often tell my writing students that the most important thing they can do when they start writing is to first spend some time in a small dark closet thinking about what they want to write. What they want to do.

I believe in the power of taking time out in a dark closet to clear your head of all those voices telling you what you should be doing instead of what you are dreaming of doing. Even worse, what you should write or create. It's time well spent just listening to yourself.

So, here we are.

Surprise! This little "stay-cation" is not exactly what we thought it was going to be. It's not business as usual, and it has slipped into overtime. It's quite unusual, and in the shift from yesterday to today, we need to suspend planning for tomorrow.

Today is just today. It will be what you want it to be. You might have work to do, or a family to feed, or a dog to walk, or a project to finish. Whatever it is, it is what you and only you need to do.

It is now. Just now. It's not what you did or who you were yesterday or what you think you're going to do tomorrow. It's right now. This is your chance to shut out all the voices in the world telling you what you should do.

The only task at hand is learning how to live in that one beautiful moment only you have today.

Make it a kind moment. Make it a personal moment. Make it a moment to share some time with your family either in person or on the phone.

Make it a good one.

The Truth about Working from Home.

Like so many of you during COVID 19, I worked from home.

I've been a freelance writer my entire professional career, and until 16 years ago, when I bought a small office building so I could better separate my work life from my family life, I worked exclusively from home.

Initially, home was an apartment. I didn't have a roommate. Call it peace, call it privilege; it made my life doable.

My apartment office was a glorious sunroom off my living room.

I went to my sunroom to write or work. I didn't even talk on the phone in my office unless it was for business. I used the landline in my kitchen for personal calls. Likewise, I didn't take professional calls in the kitchen.

The sunroom didn't have a door, and I didn't clean it up for company or holidays or anything short of an impending fire hazard.

That fire hazard thing: always a danger. It was the '70s, life before computers and all that, and there was paper. Tons of paper. Every single draft of what I was working on, as well as all my notes and research material.

Before computers, computer files, thumb drives, scanners, and whatever, everything was paper. Lots of paper. Every six months or so, I'd take off a day and try to clear my office of drafts I no longer needed, etc.

The transition from living alone to getting married in my 30s was an adjustment. First, I had to adjust my working hours. Next, I had to find a place in our home that was mine. All mine. Sacred.

Working from home, in a shared home, is about time as well as space. Place as well as peace and quiet.

The next big shift in my life came when children arrived. Three of them. With children came a bigger social world of other parents with children. That's when I learned that if I worked from home, I needed to dress for work.

Why? Because if I dropped my kids off at school while wearing sweatpants, it gave the impression that I had the day to myself and, therefore, might be available to pick up someone else's kids after school. Or, that I would have time to bake cookies for the PTA or attend some committee meeting.

While working from home, I dressed up to walk down the hallway to my office, another sunroom, this one with a door that could be closed. Dressing for work made life with children and an office at home doable.

But only slightly. It took me several years to figure out that I had to prioritize the various demands of mother/wife/work/me time. For one, I needed to set real office hours. That is, not let my work-life drift into dinner, nor meal prep into work.

I also had to manage guilt. Laundry guilt. Perfect dinners guilt. The get your homework done/diligent mother guilt. Not to mention, the *Better Homes and Gardens* house guilt.

Zoom forward to today.

For more and more people, our homes are now our offices for the foreseeable future. Everyone seems to be invited to drop by or Zoom in: your family, your co-workers, your editor, your readers, your boss, and your friends.

Which is even more reason why you should:

A) Have a place of your own to work, even if it is a corner in your bedroom or some closet you've gerrymandered into an office.

B) Cell phones, iPads, and computers make it easy to let your work life creep into every corner of your life and home. Do your best to separate home life from work life. Don't try to do the laundry or make dinner during your office hours!

C) Get dressed to go to work. Be as professional as possible. Work a Monday to Friday schedule. Take off the weekends and all holidays and birthdays.

D) When your workday is over, leave your office. Turn off the electronics and give yourself and your family a break. Working from home doesn't mean you hold office hours 24/7.

WFH is, as you have quickly discovered, far from perfect. Zoom is less satisfying than having lunch with a colleague or going to a client meeting.

But all of it is manageable as long as you don't let it manage you.

The Opposite of Isolation Is Connection. Grab It! Share It!

Learning about the power of being connected all started with lunch and a box of Triscuits.

On the days when I brave going out into the world, mask on, to work in my office, I park my car, come in, shut all the doors, and work.

I don't meet people for coffee or lunch. Don't run errands. Don't hang out with my upstairs tenant. My downstairs tenant has chosen not to come into the office because her husband is immune compromised. I understand. She's worried. I don't blame her.

I work alone and I eat lunch alone. Crackers and cheese mostly and a piece of fruit. Sometimes peanut butter and crackers. You know the COVID drill. Keep it simple. Let's just get through this.

While I was waiting for my tea to boil the other day, I pulled a box of Triscuits out of the cupboard to prepare my lunch and started reading the back of the box. There it was: "Our white winter wheat starts its journey in the Thumb of Michigan, where generations of family farmers…"

I know a fourth-generation family farmer in the Thumb of Michigan. Dennis Shoemaker is married to Sue, my best friend from high school. They own 158 acres; their son, Trent, who has taken over the management of the family farm, owns 500 acres; and they rent another 1,800 acres, on all of which they grow wheat, corn for ethanol, and soybeans. Last year, Trent's 11-year-old son, Ryan, joined his father and grandfather on the farm. He drives the grain cart.

I called my friend Sue to ask if Dennis and Trent grow the wheat for my Triscuits.

The answer? They don't grow winter white wheat for Triscuits, but the softer, red wheat that is ground for bread flour.

Even before the pandemic, my husband baked most of our bread.

There it was. A connection.

That's it, isn't it? We are all looking for ways to connect.

That's what's missing in this self-isolating, careful time.

I was so delighted to make this connection. I have told everyone I know about Dennis and his farm.

I tell them about the difference in white and red wheat and that Dennis grows the wheat that we are all using these days to bake bread. Lots of bread, because we have the time and the need to feel creative.

Connections.

A couple of days later, another great friend, Eric Woodall, delivered a container of fudge to our door. Magical stuff, indeed. It came with a delicious story about connection.

His grandmother, Louise Woodall, was a great mystery fan, and the recipe she used to make her fudge came from the "Murder She Wrote" cookbook.

Louise used a certain pot to make her fudge. No one in Eric's family was able to make the fudge the way she made it. Then one time, his brother finally succeeded, and she gave him her special pot. Unfortunately, during some move or another, he lost the pot.

Eric recently bought a pot on eBay just like his grandmother's lost pot. Now, he can make fudge just like she did.

He sent me an email with his story saying he feels his grandmother smiling down on him when he makes her fudge.

"We had a special bond," he says.

Connections.

We have a long winter ahead and much care to take with each other as we struggle to contain the pandemic and heal our country.

It's time to reconnect with friends and family. Not in person, perhaps, but through letters, phone calls, and food.

Share a recipe with a friend. Tell a story about where it came from. Connect.

Every time you bake a loaf of bread, whisper a thank you to my friend Dennis and his son who grew the wheat for your bread flour.

Then, cross your fingers and make a wish that someone you know leaves a box of fudge at your door and tells you about finding a candy pot, just like the one their grandmother used.

If there ever was a time, now is the time, to make a batch of cookies, cook up a pot of melt-in-your-mouth fudge, bake a loaf of bread, or any other family recipe that makes you feel connected, and share that delicious connection with a friend.

Give Yourself a Medal.

We are nearly one year and counting with COVID, working from home, homeschooling, wearing a mask, worrying about every cough and sneeze, ordering groceries online to avoid going into a store with people who might infect us, social distancing, cooking and eating three meals at home every day, celebrating holidays at home alone, Zooming, Zooming, Zooming until you just want to crawl under the covers and sleep until it's over.

There have been good days and bad days for everyone. However, no one is going to pat you on the back for the good things you've done today or forgive you for not making your bed or "going to work" in pajamas from the waist down and in some semblance of work clothes from the waist up, albeit wrinkled and perhaps not that clean. I mean, if you're not going outside, how dirty can your clothes get?

Bottom line: Whatever petty crimes you've committed by giving up on cultural norms and occasionally wallowing in a wee bit of self-pity and de-pression (or maybe more than a wee bit) are yours to keep.

Hang in there, grasshopper, there are many more months to go, but all is not lost.

The time has come to give yourself a medal.

I hereby declare this month and every other upcoming month, as the Month of Ordinary People Who Have Persisted in this Daunting Pandemic and Deserve to be awarded the Coveted Medal of Valor.

Check the list and see if you qualify. FYI, you only need to have done one thing on the list today to receive your medal:

You got up this morning and got dressed even though you didn't have anywhere to go.

You made your bed and brushed your teeth.

You did not eat left over cold pizza or store-bought cookies for breakfast. Instead, you made yourself a cup of tea and a couple slices of toast.

You called your children, your parents, or a friend, just to check on them and say hello.

You put on a mask and took a walk around the block.

You "went to work" virtually and got something done. No big deal done, just something.

You homeschooled your children and helped them get through at least one lesson on the list for today.

You did something to help someone else.

You put all the dirty dishes into the dishwasher, ran it, then put the clean dishes away.

Instead of mindlessly surfing the web for most of the morning, you read an article from start to finish about something other than: A) the pandemic, B) politics, C) some scary bit of coming doom. (Articles about penguins, how to make the perfect apple pie, or an article about the world outside your own world qualify.)

You did something, anything, that you have been meaning to do but didn't have the time to do before COVID when you were too busy doing things to take care of everything. This includes sewing on a button, painting your bathroom, or learning how to bake bread.

You washed your face, combed your hair, looked at your reflection in your bathroom mirror and decided you didn't look half bad for someone your age. In fact, you looked darn good.

You smiled. Better yet, you laughed at something. Perhaps, you laughed at yourself. Laughing at yourself would give you a bonus point.

Last, but not least: you got through your day with a slightly lighter heart and a sense of grace.

Congratulations. Find a medal, pin it on, and wear it with pride.

A Coveted Medal of Valor could be an old Boy Scout pin, a gaudy piece of costume jewelry your grandmother left you, or even a "Kiss Me I'm Irish" St. Patrick's Day button.

I bought my Medal of Valor at a sidewalk sale, long before I'd ever heard of COVID. It cost a dollar. I didn't even know it was an official award pin until I found it in my drawer and put it on the other morning. That's when I noticed the label on the bottom of the little plastic box it came in says: Bronze Award Pin.

I wear it to remind myself that it's not so easy to make it through every day, day after day, 24/7, mask on, social distancing, three meals a day at home, while no longer feeling the miracle of zoom in Zooming.

Put on your pin and wear it with pride. We've still got a long way to go, but we will get there.

You Had Me at Stressed and Root-Bound.

Dear 2020,

How you continue to surprise me. The sansevieria, aka snake plant/ mother-in-law's tongue, rarely produces a bloom. In fact, it only does so when it is mildly and continually stressed. This normally happens when the plant becomes rootbound.

Last week, for the first time ever, mine bloomed.

I have owned this plant for maybe 25 years. When you have something around for that long, you forget when you bought it, found it, or whether someone gave it to you. I'm pretty sure I bought it. I happen to like sansevieria. I've repotted this plant at least three times. My husband religiously waters it once a week.

It has never bloomed before now.

Sansevierias only bloom when they are mildly and continually stressed. And rootbound.

That's one hell of a metaphor for 2020.

Driving home from work yesterday, I listened to an interview about burnout. Here's a short list of burnout symptoms: becoming critical or cynical at work; having to drag yourself to work and having trouble getting started once you get there; becoming irritable with co-workers; low energy; feeling disillusioned and dissatisfied.

Hmmm. Sound familiar?

How's that working from home going for you?

Ask ten people if they are feeling stressed, and I'm willing to bet at least nine of them will say yes. And that's just the folks who still have a job.

It's hard to even imagine what it must feel like right now to have lost a job, lost a business, lost a home, or lost a loved one. It's staggering.

In addition to moving our offices home, from kindergarten to college, millions of students are going to school virtually this year … at home. Thousands of kitchen tables have been turned into work/school central. Parents all around the world are brushing up on math, world history, and grammar while trying at the same time to maintain some type of professional life with their jobs.

As if that's not enough, there's that root-bound thing.

Summer vacations are cancelled. Playdates are iffy. Dinner with friends … nope. Even going to the grocery store presents some obstacles, including standing in line six feet apart while waiting to be allowed into the store.

Then there's that stubborn sansevieria bloom.

Is it possible to bloom in all of this?

Right now, we have two choices: despair and stay in bed or get up one more time and get through another day with some grace. Trapped in the root-bound restrictions of COVID, most of us are not exactly blooming.

Truth be told, the spiky white flower of the sansevieria is never going to make it into someone's bridal bouquet.

Instead of trying so hard to bloom, let's cut ourselves and each other some slack. Let's make a vow to call a friend when we feel like the day, the moment, the work, the kids, the whatever are just too much. Instead of crumpling up on the couch, tell yourself a walk would be better, even if it's just a walk around the block.

Check on those you love: call your parents, your brothers, your sisters, your best high school friend, or your elderly neighbor who is living alone. Reach out. Be kind with each other. Get some sleep. Laugh. Pull a few weeds. Repot a plant. Ask your neighbor for a cutting from their prized begonia. Begonias are easy to root. All you need is one leaf and a glass filled with water. Got a spider plant that is overgrown with spider babies? Cut a few and share them with your friends.

There's a healing power in knowing you can grow something. It doesn't have to be beautiful or particularly luscious or successful; whatever it is you want to grow just needs to sprout and show some form of hope and a new life.

I think that's the best we can do right now. We can sprout. Let's sprout and call it blooming.

Looking for a Little Leavening in a Quarantined World?

Let them eat bread...if they can find flour and yeast!
Toilet paper wasn't the only thing in short supply during the early quarantined days of COVID.

If you could get to the store early enough, you could buy bread, but you couldn't find yeast.

It seemed that everyone in their first few weeks of confinement had decided to take up bread baking. This was not a bad thing. In fact, it was a kind of good thing. Bread baking is meditative. It engages all the senses. It takes time.

We had time and no place to go. Time to read. Time to figure out how to Zoom. Time to connect with friends. Time to nap. Time to mow the lawn. As well as time to bake bread, or at least to give baking bread a try. If you've never baked bread before, it's a bit tricky, but it is worth it for the glorious way it makes your house smell.

My husband is a bread baker. Always has been, and he's proud of it. When he was a professor and teaching full time, he didn't bake bread every day, but he almost always baked bread when we had company for dinner. But now, in his retirement and during our COVID confinement, he has time. He bakes bread for us, not every day, but many days.

Eventually, he ran out of yeast. So, he did what everyone in their fragile right mind was doing at that moment: he searched the Internet for a yeast source.

The search took the better part of a week of poking around here and there before he got lucky. At first, he found some yeast, but all the information was in Japanese and the language barrier made the transaction seem a bit risky. He wasn't sure what he would be ordering. Then, he struck gold.

He found a source, in English. However, there was, as there often is, a catch. He had to buy in bulk. Like two pounds of yeast. Without hesitation, he ordered it. Thirty-five dollars including shipping, and obviously worth it if you had time on your hands and loved to bake bread.

Why two pounds? His new-found two-pound gold mine of yeast was meant for commercial bakeries.

Let me break this down for you. You know that little package of yeast you get at the grocery store? The one that you use to make one loaf of bread? That's just over ¼ of an ounce of yeast.

Do the math. There are potentially four loaves of bread in every ounce of yeast. There are 16 ounces to the pound, multiplied by two pounds…and you suddenly have the potential of baking 128 loaves of bread.

There were only two of us sheltering in place at home. Between breakfast and sandwiches for lunch, we might use one and a half loaves of bread a week. That's about 78 loaves of bread a year.

I like bread. In fact, I love homemade bread. But 128 loaves of bread?

I don't know about the rest of you, but, sure as another loaf of bread is rising in the pan ready to be baked, I sincerely hope the curve of this disease will flatten, folks will get vaccinated, continue to be cautious and wear masks so we can go out to coffee shops and restaurants, concerts and movies, as well as share dinner with friends.

Perhaps, even take a trip to the grocery store to pick out some produce and buy a couple small packets of yeast.

P.S. We shared the yeast and spread the joy of homemade bread, and by the end of the first ten months of COVID, we ordered another two pounds.

Turns out, it's really good yeast.

It's More Complicated Than Just Taking Off Your Mask.

I usually have nightmares before talking in front of a crowd. That's just the way I'm wired.

I recently had an event at Quail Ridge Books, a local independent bookstore. It was the first in-person event I had done in more than a year and the first in-store author event the bookstore had hosted since COVID. The stakes were high on both sides of the fence.

My fourth novel, *The Inevitable Past*, came out just as life was locking down in 2020, and every in-person event for that book was canceled. So, I decided I would piggyback *The Inevitable Past* onto the launch of my latest novel, *A Musical Affair*, and make it a literary twofer.

Quail Ridge agreed to my idea of a dual launch and settled on a date we both felt might be safe, or at least safe enough. I wanted to be sure I would be fully vaccinated for the event, and they wanted their entire store staff to be vaccinated, as well.

By the time the event rolled around, the CDC had declared it was safe for vaccinated folks to take off their masks and step back into the world. This announcement upped the ante on anxiety for everyone involved.

The bookstore limited the number of attendees to 25, suggested people wear masks if they felt more comfortable, and announced the event would observe social distancing. To accommodate social distancing, attendees had to register and were assigned seating, with several empty chairs in between self-designated groups.

Before I tell you that 32 people showed up eager to buy books and listen to an author talk, let me tell you about my pre-event nightmare. It went something like this and replayed throughout the night in case I didn't get it the first time around: After I was introduced and started speaking, a group of rowdy men in hockey jerseys came into the store, took possession of all the empty chairs, turned the chairs around so their backs were to me and sat down. One of the staff members then rolled a large television set to the back of the room and turned on the hockey game. I asked the staff member what was happening. She told me the Hurricanes, the local professional hockey team, were in the playoffs. She added that this was an important game, and the bars were closed because it was Sunday, so there was nowhere else for these men to watch the game. She suggested I should continue with my presentation and just talk a little louder.

Let me break the nightmare down for you.

1. The Hurricanes were, in fact, in the playoffs that Sunday afternoon. I would never ever kid myself that a book launch would or could demand a larger audience than almost any sports event excerpt perhaps competitive shuffleboard. A literary event on the day of a major sporting event didn't have a chance of drawing a large enthusiastic audience.

2. It had been more than a year since I had done an in-person event. It was also the first time in a very long time since I had been inside a building without wearing a mask with anyone other than our family and, most recently, a few doubly vaccinated friends.

3. I was pretty darn sure, masked or unmasked, that a roomful of Caniacs, as the fans are called, did not fit neatly into my comfort zone.

Bottom line: Even if the CDC says you might be able to take off your mask and attend public events once you're doubly vaccinated, it is going to take some time before many of us are going to find a comfortable place back in the world of unmasked strangers.

I've taken off my mask but carry one in my purse just in case the situation at hand calls for one. Whenever I go somewhere, I sit in my car before getting out so I can determine if people are wearing masks or are going about their business as though the world is fair and square and safe again. Even if no one is wearing a mask, I often decide to put one on if I'm feeling at all uncomfortable or vulnerable.

Feeling safe is an individual thing, and it strikes me that we are going to have to be tolerant of others as they too try to figure out what works for them. It won't be the same for everyone.

This task of going about our business as usual is going to take time, and maybe a few more nightmares.

What's Your Breaking Point? I Found Mine While Waiting on Hold.

I've always wondered what my breaking point would be: that moment when I would hit the wall and lose it.

I found it.

It all fell apart when I had spent nearly three hours on hold trying to get a replacement backup battery for my office AT&T U-verse system. Before I go off on a rant, let me also say that AT&T has the worst on-hold music ditty ever. I mean *ever*.

One could argue that it wasn't just AT&T that brought me down, that perhaps it was the culmination of enduring four years of political unrest and chaos that played out 24/7, coupled with a worldwide pandemic for which we were totally unprepared. That maybe wearing a mask, socially isolating, working from home, ordering groceries online, spending holidays alone, not going anywhere with anyone, or doing anything, not to mention mourning the loss of family and friends could be enough to take me over the edge.

Like so many others I know in the same situation, I have managed to push through all that and keep going.

Until this morning.

You never know when someone is going to get on your last nerve. Nor can you predict what is going to light your fuse, mess with your head, make you explode.

It often involves some intense feeling of frustration, a creeping realization that you are now involved in a situation that you cannot, despite your intelligence, diligence, or good intentions, maneuver with any sense of grace.

When I discovered that my backup battery for my Internet/security system was dead, my first and most logical move was to call AT&T, the company that sold me my backup system.

Because of an "unusual high volume of calls," I was first on hold with AT&T for nearly an hour. When I eventually got through, the technician told me that I needed to speak with Belkin (the battery backup system AT&T sold me) regarding a replacement.

I foolishly felt I was getting somewhere and was about to close in on a solution. When I finally got through to Belkin, they informed me that they had cut ties with AT&T six years ago and no longer made the Belkin backup battery, that what I needed to do was go back to AT&T and request a modem upgrade.

Easy peasy.

I spent another hour on hold with AT&T. The service technician I was at last able to talk with informed me that the router I have has a battery backup in it and all I needed to do was unplug the Belkin system. Wisely, I asked him to stay on the line while I did as he instructed.

When I unplugged the Belkin battery, I lost the Internet, along with my security system.

Oops.

That's when the technician asked me to look at the bottom of my router and find the "door" to the battery for the system. I removed the door and, low and behold, there was no battery there.

So, I asked if they would please send me a battery. It was clear the system required something other than a typical AA battery.

Answer: no. They no longer provide batteries for their systems.

Then, I did what Belkin asked me to do, I asked for an upgrade.

Answer: no. My modem was working just fine, and for my information, the new modem would come without a backup battery, as well.

What kind of battery did I need to buy for my system?

He didn't know.

He put me on hold. At this point, I had been on hold for a total of three hours.

When he came back, he said no one knew.

That's when I asked to speak to a supervisor.

So, the right thing to do now is to apologize to "Joe," the supervisor. That's the name he gave me. No last name. Just Joe. And, no, he couldn't give me his direct line number. And, no, they didn't have a way to give me a battery and, no, he didn't know what kind of battery would work in the system they had sold me.

That's when I lost it. I didn't use any bad words, I just read him the opening of this post. You see, I'd been on hold long enough by then that I had had time to think about what might be happening to other people trying to get a backup battery for their AT&T modem or some other piece of failed equipment.

I had time to start writing.

I'd like to think I lost it for all of you. For everyone on hold everywhere.

What Do You Want to Do for the Rest of Your Life?

What have you done during COVID to take care of yourself? Has the uncertainty of the pandemic reshaped how you think about the rest of your life? How will your life change when you can at last take off your mask?

I once wrote a column about turning 70, titled: "If You Have the Privilege of Being Seventy, Don't Waste It."

The column was focused on ways we can and should give back from this lofty decade of wisdom and experience. No question. Seventy is not the time to sit back and do nothing. It's a golden age of giving back. A time to live a rich life by enriching the lives around us.

As I round the corner on 72, I feel the need not to revise but to expand on being seventy.

So much has happened in the last two years. For almost everyone, it has been a time of uncertainty, isolation, and frustration. We've been separated from our friends and families. Many of us have had to move our work lives into our homes, repurposing dining rooms along with clearing closets and basements in order to construct make-shift home offices. Some have had to become homeschool teachers while being home office workers, homemakers, and caretakers. We've all Zoomed holidays, birthdays, weddings, and even funerals.

We've given up traveling, dining out, shopping in stores, going to coffee shops, visiting museums, watching movies on the big screen, taking classes in person, going dancing, and spending time with friends and family. It's been exhausting. Yeah, yeah, I know, thank goodness for Netflix and Zoom…I don't know about you, but I'm about Netflix-Zoom-Roomed out.

I had a dream the other night that I had managed to go to law school during the pandemic. Hey, I had the time, why not? In any case, in my dream, I breezed through law school, aced the Bar Exam, and received a beautiful gold foil stamped certificate in the mail to prove it. I put it on my desk (always a bad choice…even before COVID, my desk was a constant disaster). I couldn't wait to show it to my family and friends. When one of my doubly vaccinated friends dropped by, I told her all about law school, but when I went to my desk to get my certificate, the one I found did not say I passed the bar. Instead, it said: Congratulations, you have lived a good life.

Had I? Had I made it a good life for those around me? Was it a good life for me? Had I done what I wanted? More importantly, what did I want to do for the rest of my life?

Good question.

Whether you're turning 22, 42, 52, or 72 this year, one thing COVID has brought into clear focus for each of us is that no one really knows how much time they have to do what they want to do: to follow their dreams or their bliss or whatever it is that motivates them. Perhaps it's time to follow the sage advice of the airlines and put on our own oxygen mask and take care of ourselves first, so we will have the strength and grace we need to look after our children, our spouses, or our friends.

What's your oxygen mask? Mine is time. Time and space. The two of them work together for me. Not more time necessarily, but quality time. Slow time. Unrushed time where I can have the space to think and dream. I have always been a doer and a helper, and it is hard for me to stop doing and helping others in order to take time to sit still and dream my own big dreams.

During this shutdown/pared-down time, I have been working on that sitting still thing. In fact, I've spent quite a bit of time being still, thinking about what I want to do for the rest of my life.

This brings me to being vaccinated and taking off the mask. We're not to "normal" yet, whatever normal is going to be. But here's the good news: We've still got time to think about what we want to do with the rest of our lives.

What do you want to do when you can at last take off the mask and live your big, beautiful life again?

Company in the Time of Being Vaccinated.

Ten minutes after we got our second vaccination, my husband began making his list of everyone he wanted to invite to our home for dinner. Only two people at a time, both doubly vaccinated, but really?

I could hardly catch my breath.

It had been more than a year since anyone had come into our home. It's complicated. Rumbling right beneath the undercurrent of fear of close contact with other people *inside* our house was the startling realization that during the past 12 months, perhaps we hadn't indulged in much housecleaning beyond keeping dirty dishes washed, laundry done and folded, and the floors swept.

We hadn't, as so many articles suggested, dug into the back of our closets to get rid of things we didn't need and/or want, sorted through that pesky junk drawer in the kitchen or even engaged in some deep cleaning ritual. We also hadn't decorated for Christmas, other than hanging a wreath on our front door, or considered doing something as bold as painting a wall or cleaning our oven.

In short, we survived. We worked at home, stayed at home, ate all our meals at home, and muddled through with as few squabbles and as much grace as possible. I was fairly pleased with how well we had done.

But we hadn't dusted, at least, not much. We did run the vacuum cleaner on a somewhat regular basis, and I became a kind of neat freak about taking out the garbage and recycling, because it made me feel we had a firm grasp on living in an orderly way. Plus, the walk to the recycling bins and the dumpster was easily as satisfying as picking up the groceries we ordered online.

While we are talking about groceries, I'm happy to confess that as soon as the ten days had passed after my second vaccination, the first thing I did was double-mask and go grocery shopping. Who knew picking out cucumbers and lettuce could be so life-affirming and uplifting?

Other than figuring out what I was going to cook and how far away we should sit from each other at our dining table, I had to rewrap my head around what I should do to make our home ready for company.

Knowing that I was not alone in this dilemma, I turned to my trusty

Woman's Day Book of Household Hints. My younger brother gave it to me as a joke one Christmas. I keep it on my desk just in case I need to do something domestic. Some of the household hints are useful. Others are fodder for a good laugh. The book was originally published in 1945 and my copy was updated in 1978. Let's just say there are some great gems in this old tome.

Take the advice, offered under the headline of "General Housework," about how to manage that awkward moment when your house is a mess and some guests telephone to say they are in the neighborhood and thought they'd drop in for tea.

Here's their list of helpful hints on how to get ready for surprise last minute guests:

In the living room, stick all litter under couches and chairs. Shake out throw rugs and put over dirty spots in carpet. Wrap a towel around your arm and slide it quickly over furniture tops. In the kitchen, stack the dirty dishes in the cupboards; wipe off counters; sweep the dirt off the floor into the broom closet. Set out coffee cups, dishes, whatever will be necessary for entertaining, so you will not have to open cupboards to reveal your secrets. In the bathroom, close the curtains around the tub and put all dirty clothes in the bathtub. Close bedroom doors. Sit back and wait for the doorbell to ring.

I feel the need to point out that the book also suggests that if you don't love cleaning, the best way to boost your morale while doing housework is to wear a cleaning costume. Something crazy which you normally wouldn't have the courage to wear out of the house.

Now, there's a thought.

Can Playing a Game Prepare Us for What's Next?

I've been thinking about what our lives will be like post-COVID 19.

Which led me to have a conversation with futures researcher Elliott Montgomery, who, along with Chris Woebken, cofounded The Extrapolation Factory, an award-winning, design-based research studio for participatory futures studies. The studio develops experimental methods for collaboratively prototyping, experiencing, and impacting our individual futures.

Extrapolation, by the way, is the practice of taking a series of data points and trying to imagine, "What's next?"

Futures researchers, like Montgomery and Woebken, do not believe that anyone can predict the future. I agree. Rather, they approach the work they do as a way for anyone and everyone to think about and practice strategic foresight.

So, let's play a game. Let's call the game *What If/What's Next*.

As Montgomery explained, there is no *one* future. There are multiple futures. In fact, each of us can imagine many possible futures for ourselves based on our individual circumstances.

The various individual and collective futures any of us can imagine are actually fictional constructs we all use in order to help us shape our thoughts and make plans.

Right now, it's anyone's guess what the world will be like tomorrow, next week, next year, or post-COVID 19. But the more we think about what might be possible, the better equipped we will become at shaping our individual and collective futures.

If futures are fictional, then why not create a game or narrative that can help us build these fictional scenarios? The game could be played by one person, with your family, or on a video conference with a large group of friends. Since the choices you make in the game reflect your possible futures, you can change the rules as your game develops, and your ideas begin to grow.

Take a piece of paper and draw a large, square game board. Draw out ten squares between each corner. Label each of the corners of the board with one of James Dator's (a groundbreaking futures researcher) suggested future trajectories:

1. Continued Growth — where things are getting bigger and better.

2. General Collapse — where things diminish. Right now, we have just lived through a Collapse state.

3. Disciplined Stabilization — where change is neutralized, either through collaboration or an outside driver of change. A Discipline state, where we self-quarantined in order to flatten the curve and prevent the spread of COVID, is a good example.

4. Abrupt Transformation — where from one day to the next, things change dramatically. This is much like what we lived through at the initial onset of this pandemic.

This is a collective, cooperative, non-competitive game, so rather than individual players, the whole group plays together and moves together around the board.

The first step in playing this game is to make a couple of dozen "What If" cards by brainstorming a wide range of possible events: flood, famine, health care for all, pandemic, stock market crash, guaranteed income for everyone, etc. Build the deck based on your own hopes and fears.

Next, you will need a pair of dice.

Roll the dice and start moving. When you land on one of the corners, draw a card from the "What If" pile. Landing, for example, on Abrupt Transformation will focus the conversation about transformation responding to your "What If" scenario.

However, before you start thinking and talking, you need to roll the dice a second time. If you roll an odd number, you have to talk about what you could build or do in order to solve the problem that will cost money. If you roll an even number, you can only talk about free solutions to solve the problem. These various solutions are the payoff for the game.

As you move around the board and face various future-altering trajectories and challenging issues, try to frame your conversations in terms of what is impossible, possible, plausible, and probable.

Whether we like it or not, COVID 19 put us in the middle of the game board. It's time to start thinking and talking about what if and what's next. This is probably not the last time our lives will be upended by a pandemic or climate change.

Playing *What If/What's Next* won't predict our various futures, but it's a great way to start thinking and moving, one square at a time, toward a whole realm of potential possibilities.

Hold On: Changes Are Coming.

In a very short two weeks, I signed a contract to sell the small office building I have owned and worked in for the last sixteen years, sold my thirteen-year-old Honda Civic and bought an all-electric Nissan Leaf, and last, but far from least, sold the baby grand piano I have had for close to 40 years in order to make room for a home office/studio at our condo.

Changes.

They're coming.

COVID confined us and perhaps helped us reorganize and prioritize our preferences and our lives. Fingers crossed, this round of COVID has set us free a wee bit to forge a different way of living. For sure, it's not going to be the same. Equally, for sure, this will not be the last time that we will have to hunker down because of a pandemic, wildfires, flooding, or whatever other kind of life changing disaster comes our way.

Whether you subscribe to the notion that we are on the edge of an environmental disaster or just think that it's hot outside, the world around us and the way we live in it are changing. Every day. In real ways. We need to pay attention.

I don't know anyone who was ready for COVID or who had any idea that it would go on for this long or that it would have created as much havoc in our lives as it has: working from home, home schooling, quarantining, cancelling plans, staying home, being home, redefining our homes and how we live in them.

It is not what anyone planned for or what we envisioned would be happening at this time in our lives. It's not what we dreamed of.

Any of it. And it's far from over.

People are talking about whether they want to go back to work in the office or continue working virtually from home. I hear talk about changing jobs, rebuilding careers, taking early retirement, selling houses, downsizing, continuing to home school or not, and debating whether it's okay to fly or take a vacation.

Decisions are harder. There's more to consider. Almost everyone agrees whatever comes next won't be the same as what came before. Life is different.

Whether you are vaccinated or not, caution seems to be the mode of decision making these days. Caution, along with confusion. Clarification would be great. A guaranteed future would be frosting on the cupcake. Good luck finding the cupcake!

One thing we have learned over these last long months is that there are no guarantees, and somehow, we need to find a way to deal with the uncertainty of that.

While floundering around deciding what to do after I was doubly vaccinated, I decided I should do more than just go to the grocery store rather than order online, so I signed up for the first art class I could find that was in person, not online.

Which took me to a local art center and a class on making a tunnel book. Look it up, I didn't know what it was either, I just knew I needed something new to do.

During the first class, the instructor mentioned that she had recently given up her big studio and downsized to a small cooperative studio, which meant she had to reckon with a lifetime of collecting beautiful handmade papers and art supplies.

I was beginning to wrestle with a similar situation of my own, selling my office/studio and moving my artwork and my writing world to the space my baby grand piano once claimed (more on that later), so I was interested in what she had to say and how she managed the change.

During the move, she said, she realized that she no longer had to hoard all the beautiful papers and paints she had collected during her lifetime of making art. It was time to let go and use them. Share them. Let them not be so precious.

I loved the generosity of her statement. The idea that the things we have are better used and shared than hoarded.

What is precious in this new life is the moment, the sharing, and the creating.

It's time to change the way we spend both our riches and our days.

PART FOUR

GOOD QUESTION

What Does Pride Have to Do with It? Everything.

I grew up in a factory town. The rust belt. Strikes, layoffs, and change-overs that took paychecks away. The United Automobile Workers. Jimmy Hoffa and the Teamsters. The whole deal.

The flipside of the complications of factory life was the pride my friends' fathers felt that the work they did allowed them to provide a good life for their families. That ability to work hard and provide a good life developed a sense of pride and a shared purpose and belief that they really were the ones who kept the world turning.

When the emphasis in manufacturing shifted in our country from large machinery to IT and computers, coal mines and factories started closing. U.S. plants were moved to other countries where there were cheaper workers. The factories that remained here were automated. Layoffs became permanent. The good times rusted, leaving many in our country feeling disenfranchised and robbed.

Who is to blame for what happened? Let's be clear about something: the fault is not that of the workers.

In assigning blame, it is easy to point to those people who are surviving the shift away from factory work to the service industry and technology; to politicians who make the rules; and to anyone and everyone who might be living the good life previously available to those who worked on the line or in the mines. In short, they feel robbed.

As much as I embrace the message of healthcare for all and free education, the message sometimes grates on my rustbelt soul.

I know about pride firsthand. My father was blind. He did not work in the factories. Instead, he was a successful self-made man and just like the men in our community who worked in the factories, he thrived on the pride that he was able to provide for his family.

I paid my own way through college because my father refused to sign the paperwork that would make it possible for me to qualify for financial aid. He said that his personal financial worth was nobody's business. But the truth was, he viewed financial aid as some form of charity.

Consequently, if I wanted to go to school, I had to work for it. So, I did.

One could pay for college working part-time back then. You can't today. A university education costs more than most people make in a year working full time. Does free tuition for my grandchildren sound good to me? You bet it does. Does it sound like a handout? Like some liberal is telling me I can't take care of my own family. A little.

My mother worked with the police and fire departments as a volunteer and coordinated a social service agency called Project Fish. It was a precursor to the local Food Bank. As soon as we were old enough to drive, we were given the job of delivering food boxes to people's homes.

All during high school and when I came home from college for Christmas and Easter, I delivered hundreds of boxes to neighbors that couldn't make mortgage payments because of strikes and layoffs in the local factories. I'd ring the bell, put the box of food on the porch, then leave.

I didn't want to have to be thanked by the families, by people I went to school with every day. I didn't want to be seen as better.

Knowing that my mother ran Project Fish out of our dining room was a double sting for many folks in the community: they didn't want to accept or acknowledge that a blind man's family was better off than they were. They were somewhat shamed by the situation. They were able-bodied and he wasn't. For them, there was something very wrong with that picture.

I never ever talked about Project Fish to anyone. No one knew, not even my best friend, that I was the one who delivered the food boxes.

What I learned growing up was how fragile a world of pride could be: both my father's pride for having defied the odds as a blind person and the pride of the people who worked in the factories and believed the work they did made America great.

Am I afraid that the tension between those who need and those who have has become not only a dividing line but might also trigger violence?

Yes. It's explosive.

Pride might be the tallest, thickest wall there is to keeping people from understanding and helping each other.

Instead of blaming liberals for everything that is wrong in the world or believing that those who proudly don a red baseball cap are less than, it's time to climb that wall of pride from both sides and build something better than what we now have. Otherwise, I'm afraid we will persist together in hate and as a result, we won't survive as a nation.

How Can You Resist the Chaos and the Clatter?

There is a certain power in resisting. Letting go of the rope others keep trying to throw around you in order to entangle you in their craziness.

Not my monkey, not my show.

A good motto. But one I've struggled with the past three years, and most particularly, during these dark and difficult last six months, RBG's death, the rush to replace her, and, let me not forget... the 2020 election.

After the 2016 election, I wanted the White House Press Corps to resist reporting on every crazy remark, every scathing action, every bit of chaos and craziness that rolled from the White House Press podium into their laps.

I believed that if they didn't make a big deal about all of it, it might calm down. That there was a chance, a slim one, but a chance, if center stage were jerked away, that the chaos would evaporate, and good things might come from this administration. That didn't happen.

It's easy to sit on the sidelines calling the shots. But it's rather arrogant to think we know what's really going on. What forces are at work.

It's tempting to poke fun about the chaos. To get alarmed. To think that you are the only one who has dug deeply enough to know the truth. It's hard not to raise your voice. Shout others down in order to be heard over all the chatter and clatter.

A couple of years into this administration, I started embroidering on fancy linen handkerchiefs. One word. Just one word: resist.

Resistance has long been a battle cry for women everywhere.

I came to embrace and enjoy embroidery late in life. I don't do anything fancy or fussy like doilies or flower-adorned tea towels. Instead, I taught myself how to embroider cursive writing freehand. The work of forming the letters one stitch at a time gave me a chance to think about what I wanted to say.

After so many years of meeting deadlines, of writing like my hair was always on fire, embroidering was a way to slow down what I wanted to say.

Right now, I am resisting the urge to post or comment on anything remotely political. I've been burned too many times by info bots, by people I went to high school with, by members of my extended family who don't share my political views. There's no purchase in it. No gain. No start of a real conversation, just a raging volley of words that fan the flames.

Posting political quips on the Internet does not calm nerves or resolve divides. In fact, it only serves to open the door to an even darker divisive place.

I've given up shouting. Now I delete. Sometimes I unfriend. Always, I try my Sunday best not to make a snarky comment on someone else's post. I have to admit it's tempting to say something snide, but deep down, I believe the person I have perceived as deceived, shallow and okay, maybe even racist, didn't post their views because they wanted me to react in a demeaning or critical way. They posted because they believed they were right.

We all do.

That's the funny thing about what's going on in our country right now. We all think we are right.

What's right? Hard question. WWJD and all that.

Our elected officials, whether they are altruistic or self-serving, have a certain amount of control over our lives and the world we live in. I don't know about you, but I get up every morning a bit terrified to read the news, wondering what's going to happen next. I hate feeling hopeless.

Bottom line: I refuse to become one of those voices that helps normalize what is going on. To think there's nothing I can do.

Whenever hope starts slipping away, I take out another handkerchief and start embroidering the one word that rings true for me: resist.

Now, more than ever, it's important that we all resist the temptation to quit.

Because there is something we can do.

Vote, not just in this election, but every election, be it local, statewide or national.

It's time to make our wishes known and our voices heard.

Is It Time to Jump Off the Sinking Chaos Ship?

I've been thinking about Jonah lately. Most particularly, the boat he got on to avoid doing what he was called to do; the storm that threatened to destroy the boat and drown everyone aboard; his decision to jump overboard in order to save the ship; and the whale that swallowed him whole.

I realize the Bible says, "a big fish," but what other than a whale would be big enough to swallow Jonah?

That's where I get stuck.

The whale.

It's not what you think. It is rather hard to believe that one could be swallowed whole, shoes and all, without having serious bodily injury. Plus, there's that bit about being inside a large creature's stomach for three days, sloshing around in gastric juices and yesterday's lunch, without sustaining further physical damage or mental derangement. But that's not where I get stuck.

What stops me, when it comes to the whale in the story, is that Jonah had three whole days in the dark and calm of some benevolent creature's belly.

The truth is, I envy him.

Jonah got there by abandoning a sinking ship. Some might say he jumped into the storm. I think he jumped away from it.

He left it behind.

He made what he thought was a clean break, and his reward was three days of quiet and calm to think.

He didn't have a cell phone with him. There was no cable news reminding him of melting icebergs, rising oceans, and chaos-producing political decisions. No threat of another war. No new walls to keep us apart or turn away people who just need a safe place to live and raise a family. No shocking terrorist attacks or mass shootings.

Just a small dark room. Quiet. Calm. A place to be alone and think about what he had done in his life, what he had failed to do to help others, and perhaps what he should do next.

If you read of the story of Jonah, you will discover that he didn't bother to start praying to get out of the whale's belly until the third day.

That's the other thing that stops me.

When I first read that he didn't start praying until the third day, I wondered, if I were in the same situation, would I panic and start praying right away, hoping for a quick deliverance back to my old life? Or would I wait?

I would like to believe that, like Jonah, I would wait. That I would use those precious couple of days alone to think, perhaps to dream about what it was that I could do next. If I had enough courage and believed that somehow being swallowed by a whale was a divine intervention, I hope I would take the time I needed to decide just how I should proceed with the rest of my life, perhaps to do something that might quell the storm, calm the chaos, and make the world a kinder place in which to live.

The story of Jonah intrigues me, I guess, because I believe we all get a chance, even a second chance, if we only take the time we need to get away from the chaos and the rising storms around us, to think about what we might or could do next to save some small piece of the world.

It's worth reflecting on and praying about on the third day, for sure.

Do Walls Conquer or Divide?

We were living in Avignon, France in 1991 and took our three children to a resort hotel on the Costa Brava in Spain for Spring/Easter Break. Easter was early that year and no other hotels had opened for the tourist season ahead.

The day we arrived, a small fleet of buses pulled up to the hotel and several hundred recently liberated East Germans poured out. Their clothes were shabby, mismatched and out of fashion, but their faces were bright and jubilant. It was the first time in many of their lives that they had been able to travel anywhere outside of the Soviet Bloc.

Reservations at this resort hotel included breakfast and family-style dinners.

When dinner was served that first night, along with unlimited carafes of cheap red wine, the East German guests became joyously drunk. By the time the flan was served, they were out of their seats, arms linked, singing at the top of their lungs, while others in their party danced on the tables.

The hotel manager came by to apologize for their behavior.

No apologies needed. Our children were fascinated by the Germans' unbridled joy, and we were challenged to think about what their trapped lives must have been like.

The Berlin Wall went up in 1961, cutting off West Berlin from virtually all of surrounding East Germany and East Berlin. The Eastern Bloc portrayed the Wall as protecting its populations from fascist elements conspiring to prevent the "will of the people" from building a socialist state in East Germany. The Wall was opened in November of 1989 and its official demolition began in June of 1990.

Fences may sometimes make good neighbors, but high fences adorned with razor wire come with two warnings. On the side with the armed guards the warning is loud and clear, you cannot leave. On the other, the message is more subtle but still understood: Keep out, you are not welcome here.

We were in Berlin a few weeks ago. Although no longer divided, its soul is still marked by the Wall.

When the Wall came down, the reunited city left a kilometer-long stretch of the Wall in place. It stands not only as a reminder of freedoms lost and later recovered but as a ready canvas for anyone, be they artist, student, or activist, to say something. Artists come at all hours of the day and night, toting their collections of spray paints. No one stops them. Residents and tourists alike come every day to watch the artists paint their pictures and protests on the Wall. There is no censorship as to what can be written or drawn. There are no graffiti police.

In addition to this remaining piece of the Wall, there are brick paths throughout Berlin that allow you to walk the original length of the Wall and see for yourself how the city was divided and the West surrounded.

As you walk along this ghost outline, you find bits and pieces of the Wall on display, along with explanations of not only the Wall, but also the "dead" zone, the area between the high Wall and the razor wire barrier where people were shot trying to escape.

Walking the brick path, that was once the Wall, allows you to see how neighborhoods and neighbors were separated, and to feel the depth and breadth of the scar the Wall carved through this city.

We sat next to a young couple during dinner our first night in Berlin. When we asked if they were from Berlin, they replied, yes, but that they would rather claim to be from Austria where there was no Wall.

What happened in Berlin during WWII, along with the Wall that divided and dominated their city for 28 years during the Cold War, is, for young Berliners, as well as those who are old enough to remember when the Wall went up and when it came down, a shadow of shame.

In 1991, we saw first-hand what freedom meant to our fellow vacationers in Spain and left at the end of that week wondering what freedoms were lost to those on the Western side of the Wall.

There are two sides to every wall, and no matter which side you're on, something is lost, and lives get changed...forever.

Are Powerful Ancestors Hiding in Your DNA?

According to Disney, when Mulan is faced with the realization that her father is physically unable to join the Imperial Army and go to war against the Huns, she grabs his sword and puts on his armor. But, first, she visits their family shrine to call upon their ancestors to accompany her on this perilous journey.

That thing about acknowledging the ancestors and asking them to aid her on her journey is just a cultural nod to some ancient Chinese beliefs. Right?

Or is it?

Many cultures hold strong beliefs about deceased ancestors living among us, guiding us, and protecting us as we go about our daily lives. Cultural Anthropologists have documented these beliefs and the rituals surrounding them as though they are purely culturally specific and, as such are interesting in their context, but hardly applicable to the way we live our enlightened lives.

Right?

Enter Ancestry.com and other similar services. Our modern-day version of the ancestral shrine. The missing branches of truth on our family tree. The connection we are looking for in our search for ourselves.

If you are one of the many millions who have swabbed your cheeks or spit in a tube, then awaited the results, you are among those searching for answers. Looking for connections. Trying to make sense of who you are. Or, simply, why you have grey eyes rather than brown like your brother's.

How about, why you think and feel the way you do? Or the dreams you have? Or the fears you can't explain?

What's in your DNA beyond your grey eyes?

Science now supports the idea that there's more to your DNA than your good looks.

Epigenetics is the study of what is coded in your DNA beyond obvious physical traits. This scientific study is focused on how traumas or other dramatic events in the lives of your ancestors have the potential to build an additional layer of information onto your DNA. This overlaid coding of information shapes how your underlying genes express themselves. Along with your genes, this epigenetic coding can then be passed on, sometimes skipping a generation.

In other words, the imprint of your grandmother's life experiences can become part of your responses to your life experiences.

Put more broadly, your ancestors' experiences, their joys, fears, triumphs and failures, might imprint on and shape your personality, bequeathing anxiety or resilience by altering the epigenetic expressions of your genes.

The shrine of your ancestors is hidden in your DNA. The family members who have gone before you are within you and are shaping your thoughts, your dreams, and perhaps even your behaviors.

My own personal journey of visiting my ancestral DNA shrine took the form of my latest novel: *The Inevitable Past.*

In many ways, it's a ghost story. Or a thread of a story that took me on a literary journey looking for a grandmother I never knew.

My father's birth mother was found badly beaten on the train station platform in Macon, Georgia in 1902. The police who discovered her, unconscious, quite pregnant, and without any identification, took her to the Door of Hope, a home for unwed mothers. When a doctor examined her, he realized she was dying and made the decision to do a C-section to try to save the baby, my father.

Who my grandmother was, and how her life has shaped mine, has haunted me my whole life.

So, I went searching for her in the only way I knew how, by going to Macon, looking for threads of her story, finally putting together a life for her that made sense for me.

It was an odd journey, not unlike discovering, via Ancestor.com, some deeply hidden family secrets.

The stories locked in our DNA are fascinating. If you can think of your life as a living shrine of your ancestors, you, like Mulan, can gain insight into how recognizing them can give you self-awareness, strength and courage.

When I finished researching and writing a purely fictional account about a grandmother I never knew, I came to think of my own DNA as a shrine where traces of my grandmother, as well as other ancestors, reside and shape my life.

While writing *The Inevitable Past* I came to understand and believe in ghosts: fingerprints of the past that shimmer and shine not only in the color of my eyes, but the dreams I have and the way I live.

When my sister read the book, she called me.

"At last," she said, "we have a grandmother. Thank you."

Harry Potter vs. J.K. Rowling. Where Do You Stand?

DISCLAIMER: *Yes, I do know that ugly, dark thing about J.K. Rowling making statements that many consider transphobic. I'm sorry about that. It's her problem. People are allowed to have their opinions and attitudes. I don't have to agree with them, but I also don't have to throw away the good someone has done just because I don't share their opinions and attitudes.*
READ ON IF YOU DARE!

Somewhere around week 13 of COVID confinement, I had tired of being quarantined, tired of being blindsided by the daily tsunami of bad news and political chaos and was brain-dulled by interacting with folks through Zoom.

That's when I discovered a complete set of the Harry Potter books that had once belonged to our children. Halfway through the first of the seven volumes, I tumbled into the Pensieve and found a few hidden truths, along with some insights on good and evil, us and them.

Let me break it down for you. The issue of good vs. evil/us vs. them depends entirely upon your point of view.

Remember that.

Every time we see ourselves as us/good, the very same people we are denigrating as them/evil define themselves as us/good. Which makes us them/evil.

Like I said, point of view.

Which is not to say that there isn't evil in the world. There is. Sometimes, it's obvious, and other times, it's cloaked in fast-talking rhetoric that obscures not only the truth but the motivation behind the lie as well.

Given all the chaos and confusion going on right now in the world, I'd love to have the power to mix up a batch of veritaserum. Three drops of the clear, tasteless liquid would be enough to force the drinker to answer questions truthfully.

Who is on your "would like to hear the truth for once" list? President past and present? The CDC? How about the weatherman? Or your mom?

Reading through the seven volumes of Harry Potter's education made me keen to take Professor Trelawney's divination class. Don't dismiss her too quickly; she did get it right five times out of ten, which is like batting 500 for most fortune-tellers.

Wouldn't you like to be able to see into the future and know what's really going on with climate change? The various wars and conflicts around the world and in our country? How about when it's going to be safe again to go back to work, travel, eat in a restaurant or plan a wedding?

If we knew, really knew for sure, that everything is going to be okay in the end, even if it will be changed, I think all the uncertainty in the world and the ever-changing world problems would be easier to swallow.

What kept me reading about Harry and his friends was not any promise of happily ever after, but the shifting of good and evil. I had to pay attention.

Evil seemed to dominate life at Hogwarts, but characters who looked evil sometimes harbored hidden good, and some who appeared to be trustworthy and good had some rather dark secrets and motives.

Even Harry was good at times and impatient and rude at others. But through it all, he cared about other people. In the end, that's what saved him.

What I loved the most about the books was that although Harry and friends were born with something special, they had to go to school to learn how to use their powers. They had to study. They had to develop their skills. They had to learn patience, humility, kindness, and courage. They had to grow up.

Adulting is no fun. Adulting in these dark times is really no fun.

So, here's to Harry Potter. Thanks for growing up. It helped me see the world as a child again.

Thank you, Harry and friends, for sharing your fun and failures with me. Your story gave me much, much more than just an escape from the endless #sameoldsameold days of working from home. I got a moment to reflect on the continued struggle between us and them and between good and evil.

We are all born with special powers, particularly the power to be creative and caring.

Here's the truth: The only way to practice true empathy and caring is to open our hearts to other points of view.

Harry, you showed me that there are bumps and lumps in life, and how things that get broken can also be healed.

You also taught me that there is nothing in the world stronger than love and hope.

Thanks.

It's All About the Extended Warranty.

Please Don't Hang Up!

Her voice was cool and mechanical. I hung up. Didn't even say hello. I knew she wanted me to pay for an extended warranty on my thirteen-year-old Honda Civic.

Even after I sold the car, she kept calling.

Bless her heart.

I keep a landline at my office for my Internet service. I recently changed my phone/internet service and opted for a new unlisted phone number while I was at it. I had long ago forgotten my original landline number. I never used it and never gave it to anyone for any reason. Getting an unlisted number seemed like a possible solution to unwanted scams and solicitations.

Even though I no longer knew my old landline number, many people did…all of them overly concerned folks who didn't want me to hang up. They called because they wanted to sell me an extended warranty for my aging car.

My office phone would ring six to ten times a day with such calls. I got very adept at picking up the phone and clicking it off with my thumb, without bothering to listen to the message or losing my train of thought. It's important to always be working on expanding your skill set.

When I switched Internet services and requested a private number, I felt like I had just won the phone solicitation game with a slam dunk from the three-point line.

The quiet honeymoon of no landline calls lasted a little more than a month. Then one morning, the landline rang. I was so surprised I picked up the phone and said hello.

Big mistake. The calls began pouring in with a vengeance. They'd found me again and, as before, I'd pick them up and click them off like a pro, but that didn't stop the calls from coming. In fact, the solicitations became ever more persistent. They were on to my hang-up skills and turned up the volume on their end so the initial *Please don't hang up!* could be heard at arms-length.

A couple of days ago, the phone rang with the usual plea to *Please don't hang up!* Then just before I could mash on that button and hang up, the mechanical woman added a new twist. She told me she was calling from a secure location and that, in fact, I really should hang up IMMEDIATELY and vacate my office because I was in danger.

In danger of what, I never found out. I just hung up and kept working.

I'm here to tell you that all is well. I'm safe. Nothing happened other than I finished editing the story I was writing, and miracle of miracles, the phone hasn't rung since.

I'm hoping that last call was one of those *Mission Impossible* kind of things where the message self-destructs after 30 seconds and there's a bit of a sizzle on the line, then silence.

I can only hope.

PART FIVE

SHIFTING FORWARD TO A CLEANER, SAFER WORLD

It's Easier and Cheaper Than You Think to Be Green. It's Time to Come Clean!

It's hard not to respond to the hyped-up-online-everywhere-advertising world in which we now live. The message is loud and clear: if you're still using harsh chemicals, you're destroying the planet. In fact, every time you scrub the toilet, clean the bathtub, wash the dishes, throw a little bleach in your wash to eliminate grass stains or whiten the whites, you are personally responsible for destroying the planet.

The better crafted the message, the quicker you grab a credit card and order something, anything that will make the world and your life better.

Truth is, you already have the one thing that will make all the difference in the world. It's baking soda.

Rust stains or soap scum in your sink or bathtub? Grungy grout in your shower? Pull that box of baking soda from your shelf, slice a lemon in half or pour on some lemon juice, and start scrubbing. In less time than it would take to order yet another product off the Internet, all those troubling stains, soap scum and mold in your shower disappear.

You can use lemon juice or vinegar in combination with the baking soda for the really tough stuff. Baking soda, pure and simple, is all you really need most of the time.

Baking soda has several characteristics that make it ideal for cleaning: it is a basic (as opposed to acidic) compound with a pH of 8.4 in water; it reacts with acids (such as vinegar or lemon juice) to release carbon dioxide; it is nontoxic and nonabrasive; it absorbs odors; and it reacts with other compounds as a booster. If you add a half-cup of baking soda to your heavily soiled wash, you can reduce the amount of bleach you normally use by half. In fact, if you regularly add baking soda to your wash, you will discover that your clothes stay brighter and won't need bleach.

You can cut the amount of dish soap you normally use in half by adding two tablespoons of baking soda to the water. If you do this, not only will your dishes be cleaner, but your glassware will sparkle. You can also go half and half with the soap powder you use in your dishwasher, and you'll not only have cleaner dishes, but a better smelling dishwasher.

Baking soda is completely non-toxic and breaks down quickly in water, causing no threat to aquatic life. It's also non-abrasive, so much so that it is an excellent substitute for toothpaste. Plus, it comes in a cardboard box, so the container is 100% recyclable. Having periodontal problems? Make a paste of peroxide and baking soda for brushing. You can also make an excellent mouthwash by mixing one teaspoon of baking soda in a half-glass of water to neutralize mouth odors.

Wear contacts? You can clean soft contacts with a pinch of baking soda mixed with water. Also, since baking soda is completely non-abrasive, you can use it to clean bugs and grime from your car. You can also use it to remove battery corrosion: simply make a paste of one part baking soda and one part water. Apply this paste to the battery terminals, let it sit for a few minutes then wipe away the paste and the corrosion. The baking soda neutralizes the corrosion.

To make a scrubbing paste, combine three parts baking soda to one-part water. To make a cleaning solution, use four tablespoons of baking soda to a quart of water. Need to attack a really grimed in stain? You can either make a scrubbing paste of baking soda and water or use baking soda straight from the box. When cleaning tough things like mildew, grass stains, or baked on food in your cookware, make a paste, apply, then let sit for ten minutes before you scrub.

One of the only things you can't clean with baking soda and water is wood furniture or your floors.

Don't get suckered into buying yet another "miracle" cleaning product. Put your credit card away. Besides creating a cleaner, safer environment in which to live and breathe, by using baking soda as your primary cleaning aid, you automatically eliminate dozens of plastic bottles and tubes from landfills.

Next up: Vinegar is the solution!

Vinegar: The Environmentally Safer Cleaning Solution.

Many commercially made cleaning products wreak havoc with air and water quality, not to mention that they are harsh on your hands, your home, and your wallet.

While baking soda tops my list of inexpensive environmentally friendly ways to keep bathrooms and kitchens clean, baking soda can't do it all. For instance, you should never use baking soda on wood furniture or your floors whether they're wood, tile, natural stone or linoleum.

So, what should you use?

White vinegar!

Vinegar is a solution of acetic acid and trace chemicals, typically in a mild solution of 5-20% by volume. One cup of white vinegar in a gallon of warm water is the most highly recommended and preferred cleaning solution for wood furniture and floors. It is also an effective go-to cleaner for baseboards, woodwork and windowsills. Try it on the bricks around your fireplace. You'll be amazed by the results.

Equal parts white vinegar and water is an excellent solution for removing grease on your stovetop, broiler or countertops and can be used to remove wax and grime from wood furniture. This one-to-one solution also makes a safe tick and flee spray for your dogs. Just like ticks and flees, many garden pests, including fire ants and deer, do not like the smell of vinegar and will be happy to move on to another locale if you keep the area freshly sprayed each week with this environmentally safe concoction.

You can safely use vinegar full strength on a number of household cleaning problems, including: removing ballpoint ink from walls and furniture; getting grime off of scissor blades; cleaning chrome and stainless steel; removing mineral deposits from tea and coffee pots; getting rid of stubborn toilet stains (pour full strength into the toilet and let sit overnight before flushing); treating food and sweat stains on clothing; disinfecting wooden cutting boards, counter tops and cooking tools in order to remove the risk of e-coli bacteria.

Add a couple of tablespoons of vinegar to your regular dish washing liquid and you'll discover that you need to use less dish soap to make dishes, glassware and flatware sparkle. Likewise, trade out bleach for a cup of vinegar in your weekly wash to not only brighten your whites and colors but also make them smell better and be static free. Use a quarter cup of vinegar regularly as the rinse agent in your dishwasher and watch your glassware shine!

There are hundreds of vinegar cleaning and household aid recipes on the Internet. My favorite bathroom cleaning solution is made by combining two cups of white vinegar with one cup of blue Dawn dish detergent. Heat the vinegar in your microwave for one to two minutes (dish water warm but not boiling) and mix in the dish detergent. Let the mixture cool then pour into a spray bottle. Spray your tub, shower or sink. Let it sit for a minute, then rinse. Your tile and tub will be free of soap scum, bathtub ring and mildew.

I keep a spray bottle of this vinegar/dish detergent combination in each of our bathrooms and regularly spray down the shower/tubs and sinks before turning on my morning shower (let the water run for a couple of minutes so the tub won't be slippery). I also have a spray bottle in my kitchen with the half vinegar/half water solution for cleaning the stovetop, countertops and cutting boards after dinner.

Caution: Never use vinegar on marble or granite countertops.

The trick to using vinegar to help you clean is to keep it handy. Put a large bottle of vinegar in the laundry room to use with the wash and another under the kitchen sink to add as the rinse solution to your dishwasher. I also like to keep a box or two of baking soda handy in the laundry room, the bathroom and the kitchen for those cleaning jobs that need an extra boost or some hard scrubbing.

Vinegar and baking soda cannot solve all your cleaning problems, but they are a good first step combo toward coming clean and going green.

Step Off the Gas!

I had been thinking about buying an all-electric car. Thinking it would be a good thing to do for the environment, but not thinking I'd do it like now. Maybe next year or the year after. Fun no-cost future thinking. Dreaming. I'd gotten as far as what color I wanted.

Then the son of a friend of ours needed a car. Something old but reliable. Maybe a bit sporty. Good tires. Low mileage.

It had taken me three years to find my last car. I'm from Detroit, where learning to drive and buying your first car are rites of passage. Cars, if you're from Detroit, are not just transportation. They are dream machines, part of your persona.

I wanted to be a REAL driver, so I learned to drive stick before I got my license, and except for that brief mother-of-small-children-minivan period in my life, every car I have owned has had a standard transmission.

My first car was a cherry red Karmann Ghia Coupe. Four on the floor stick shift, of course. Lots of fun to drive.

The car I sold to our friend's son was a thirteen-year-old champagne-colored/stick shift Honda Civic with 73,000 miles, a moonroof (I had always dreamed of owning a convertible, but in reality, I am ivory-skinned Irish and can sunburn in a summer thunderstorm, so I settled for a moonroof), a full tank of gas and a new set of tires. Sensible, but sporty in its own right.

My trusty Honda gone, my search for a new car was on.

I mentioned that cars were an essential part of a Detroit persona. Think of it like a heartbeat—a kind of private as well as public identity.

Sorry, I couldn't buy a Tesla. Teslas are top-notch, sexy, modern…all that. But not me or my bank account.

Buying an all-electric car was not about the status for me. It was my way of doing the right thing, one small change at a time.

I keep my cars for a long time. I get attached. Because I drove my last car for thirteen years, I felt I couldn't wait a dozen years or so to make the environmental commitment to go all-electric. An EV hybrid wasn't part of the equation. Mine was an all-or-nothing decision: time to let go of my past dependency on gas and oil and improve my carbon footprint.

After shopping around, I settled on an all-electric Nissan Leaf. Bright red, of course. Nissan calls it scarlet. Nice name. Perfect.

Here's what I didn't know when I switched to an electric car.

1.   It has amazingly quick acceleration. The car goes from 0-60 with a soft tap on the accelerator. It also stops quickly, so it took a few weeks to adjust my heavy gas/brake pedal driving ways.

2.   Surprise…everything in the car is run off the battery. When you turn on the AC, listen to the radio, make a call with Siri, start the car, roll down the windows, etc., you're drawing on the battery, i.e., your mileage per charge goes down. The good news: you pay more attention to the energy you are using. Not a bad thing.

3.   The car is quiet. Why does this matter? Every quiet electric car on the road contributes to the reduction of noise pollution as well as emission pollution. Unless you are backing up or driving less than 25 miles an hour (Nissan figures at such slow speeds, more than likely there would be school children or neighbors out for a stroll, and they ought to hear you approaching), your car doesn't make a lot of noise, and you don't hear a lot of noise. When I drive my husband's Prius, I'm amazed at how much noise gas-fueled cars make, even hybrid ones.

4.   My car gets around 210-230 miles per full charge, which costs about $5. We have a charging station where we live. EV charging stations are cropping up across the country, making road trips possible. It's true, there are not as many charging stations as there are gas stations, but this is changing.

What's my favorite thing about driving an electric car? I live in a less noise-polluted world. Oh yeah, and I no longer have to panic when gas breaches $3.00 a gallon. My last fill-up of my Honda (I got 210-220 miles per tank of gas…about the same as a full charge on my LEAF) cost me $27.00.

All-electric for this old Detroit babe…no brainer.

PART SIX

POSTSCRIPT

How Do You Want to Be Remembered?

One of the things I learned from living through my mother's decline with Alzheimer's is that memory is a fundamental part of the everyday of our lives. We *need* to remember.

Memory is a rather magical human trait. It allows us to share what we experience and make connections with the world and the people we care about. It is the thread that binds us to one another. Through memory, we learn to love, to trust, and to care about each other.

If we don't remember the answers to the questions, we fail the test. If we can't remember the way home, we get lost. If we don't remember to take the dinner out of the oven, it will be ruined. If we don't remember the faces of those we love and who love us, we become estranged from our lives and the lives of others. If we don't or can't remember, we have no past, no present, and no future. We are disconnected and all alone.

One of the more far-flung theories being tossed about regarding the reason our parents and grandparents are experiencing Alzheimer's in such alarming numbers is that they saw so many terrible things happen during World War II—the concentration camps, Pearl Harbor, and the dropping of the atomic bomb, not to mention the horror of the war itself—that they developed the disease in order to forget.

With Vietnam, two Gulf Wars, 9/11, too many senseless school shootings and every other tragedy we've witnessed in recent years, are we doomed to have Alzheimer's? Destined to forget?

Artists and writers have always served as scribes for humanity. They put down in lines and colors, words and songs, the things they see and feel. When we write a story, draw a picture, play music, sing a song, dance, or throw a pot, we engage in an act of memory.

We want to remember. We need to remember. Memories make us happy. They can also make us sad. But whether happy or sad, memories connect us. That is why we tell stories when we sit at our kitchen tables, why we take pictures when we travel, why we send emails to our friends.

We want to connect. We want to hold on to our memories. Because in some very fundamental way we understand that if our memories are lost, we are lost.

One of the most curious things about Alzheimer's is that when the victim has forgotten most of their memories and nearly all their language, if they hear a song that has some strong memory attached to it, whether it is the singing of the hymn *Amazing Grace* or *The Old Rugged Cross*, or even a song they once danced to with someone they loved, they can recall and call back every word of the lyrics and sing along. When they sing, their faces are no longer blank and flat, but filled with memory in a way that can break your heart—for when the music stops, the words and the memories are once again forgotten.

Some researchers have suggested we can stem the tide of Alzheimer's by keeping mentally active working crossword puzzles and reading books.

My mother read books and did puzzles until she could no longer remember how to read or knew puzzle pieces were meant to fit together.

Books and puzzles are not enough. I believe we should make art. I think we should take some time every day to pinch a pot, take a picture, write a poem, arrange a vase of flowers, bake a beautiful cake, sing a song, dance, do anything to spark the creative spirit within us that says: *This is what I see, this is what I feel, this is what I want to remember about this day.*

This is what I want you to remember about me.

9 781952 085154